# 365
## TALES OF
# Indian mythology

OM

Om Books International

This edition is published in 2006 by

**Om Books International**
4379/4B, Prakash House, Ansari Road,
Daryaganj, New Delhi 110 002
Tel :        91-11-23263363, 23265303
Fax :       91-11-23278091
e-mail :    sales@ombooks.com
            ombooks@bol.net.in
website :   www.ombooks.com

Design and Packed by: Cyber Media Services
Printed in India by Gopsons Papers Ltd., Noida.

ISBN 8-18710-746-4

# 365
## TALES OF
# Indian mythology

# Contents

*The Story of the Month:*   *Shakuntala*

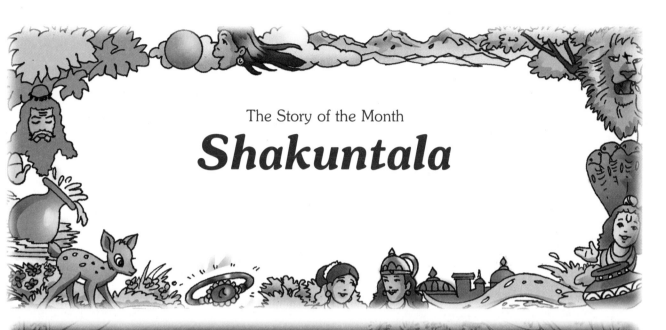

The Story of the Month
# Shakuntala

# Shakuntala

Shakuntala was a beautiful maiden who was the adopted daughter of Sage Kanva. She lived with him and her pet deer, in his hermitage in the forest. One day, Dushyanta, the king of Hastinapur, came hunting in the forest. He saw the beautiful deer and shot an arrow at it. Shakuntala found her deer whimpering in pain and tried to comfort it. Shakuntala loved the animals of the forest and her affection for the animal touched Dushyanta's heart and he asked her to forgive him for his cruelty. She forgave him but asked him to stay in the forest for a few days to tend the wounded deer. They fell in love and King Dushyanta married Shakuntala and gave her a wedding ring with his name on it. The king then left for his kingdom after promising to return soon and take Shakuntala back with him.

One day, Sage Durwasa came to Shakuntala's door. He repeatedly asked for water, but Shakuntala was lost in thoughts of Dushyanta and paid no attention. The sage was insulted and got very angry. Known for his temper, he cursed Shakuntala saying that the person whom she was thinking about would forget her.

When Shakuntala heard the curse, she was frightened and begged the sage to forgive her. The sage said that he could not take back the curse but he could change it—the person whom she was thinking about would recognize her if she showed him something he had given her.

Due to the curse Dushyanta forgot Shakuntala. After days of waiting for him to return, Shakuntala decided to go to the capital to meet him. On the way, as Shakuntala was crossing a river, her wedding ring fell into the water. A fish swallowed the ring. When Shakuntala arrived at the palace, the king did not recognize her. He

asked her to prove her identity but Shakuntala didn't have the ring to show him, as it was lost. She wept and told the king about the time he had spent with her in the forest but he couldn't remember anything. Feeling sad she left the palace.

Ashamed to return to her father's home, she started living alone in another part of the forest where she gave birth to a son. She called him Bharata. Bharata was a brave boy. He grew up among the animals of the forest and would play with wild animals.

One day at the king's palace, a fisherman brought him a

ring. He told the king that he had found the ring in the stomach of a fish that he had caught. When he found the king's name on it, he had brought it straight to him. As soon as the king saw the ring, the curse was broken and the king remembered Shakuntala. He was very upset and hurried at once to her home in the forest to look for her, but could not find her. In despair, he returned to his palace.

Few years passed. The king again went hunting in the forest. There he was surprised

to find a boy playing with a lion cub. The boy fearlessly held open the mouth of the cub and said, "O king of the jungle! Open your mouth wide, so I can count your teeth." The king went up to the boy and asked him about his parents. The little boy replied that he was the son of King Dushyanta and Shakuntala. Dushyanta was very happy to have found Shakuntala and asked the boy to take him to his mother. The family was united and Dushyanta took Shakuntala and Bharata along with him to Hastinapur.

Bharata grew up to become a great king.

# 1  The Curse

King Dasaratha, the noble and courageous descendant of the Surya dynasty, ruled over the kingdom of Kosala from the capital city of Ayodhya. He had three queens: Kausalya, Sumitra, and Kaikeyi. Dasaratha was blessed with fame, glory, peace, and prosperity. But he had one great sorrow; he did not have any children.

One day, King Dasaratha went hunting in the forest. He and his men roamed the forest when suddenly they heard a gurgling sound in the distance. Thinking it to be an animal drinking water, the king shot his arrow in that direction.

When Dasaratha came to the spot he found a youth lying seriously wounded by the arrow. He was Shravana Kumar, the only son of an old and blind couple. He had come to fetch water to quench the thirst of his parents resting in the forest. Shravana carried his old parents on his shoulders, in a palanquin, wherever he went.

Even while dying, Shravana could only think of his helpless parents. He held Dasaratha's hands and asked him to take the pitcher of water to his parents. Unsuspectingly the old couple drank the water, but an extremely sorrowful Dasaratha could not withhold the truth.

He told Shravana's parents how he had unknowingly killed their son.

Shocked by the news, the grieving parents cursed Dasaratha with *putrasoka*, which meant that he would go through the same agony of child loss.

Years later, this curse led to the exile of Rama, and Dasaratha suffered the pain of separation from his favourite son.

---

# 2  The Prediction

Kansa, the ruler of Mathura, was a greedy and ruthless man. He was a tyrant and the people of Mathura were terrified of him.

Kansa loved his sister, Devaki, dearly. When Devaki was getting married, Kansa decided to be the charioteer of the bridal chariot and drive Devaki and her husband, Vasudeva, through his kingdom.

While driving the chariot, Kansa heard a voice from the heavens above, "You fool, your days on earth are nearing their end!"

Kansa was startled. The voice roared again, "The eighth child of Devaki will kill you." Kansa wanted to kill his sister but Vasudeva begged Kansa to spare them and promised to surrender all his children to Kansa.

Kansa agreed but immediately threw them in prison. He killed the first six children as soon as they were born but Krishna and Balarama were saved by Vasudeva's quick thinking. Years later the prophecy proved true and Krishna killed Kansa.

# 3 Ravana

Ravana was the king of demons and the ruler of Lanka. He had ten heads and twenty arms. Ravana was a great devotee of Lord Shiva and had been granted many boons by him. Brahma had also granted him a boon by which he could not be killed by any god or demon. However, Ravana forgot to ask for protection from men or animals.

Ravana was blessed with many supernatural powers such as flying and becoming invisible, but this also made him very proud. He misused his powers and the gods felt it was necessary to destroy him. Since only a human could kill Ravana, Lord Vishnu incarnated himself as Rama, prince of Ayodhya. With the help of an army of monkeys, Rama went to Lanka and killed Ravana, symbolising the triumph of good over evil.

# 4 Prahlad

In the olden days, giant demons were called *daityas*. Hiranyakashyap was the king of the *daityas* and he wanted to conquer the world and be worshipped by everyone.

Hiranyakashyap's son, Prahlad, was a devotee of Lord Vishnu. Hiranyakashyap did not like this but Prahlad was unmoved in his devotion. So, Hiranyakashyap decided to kill Prahlad. He tried to get snakes to crush Prahlad but Prahlad prayed to Vishnu and was saved. Then Hiranyakashyap tried to throw Prahlad from a cliff but Prahlad escaped. Finally, Hiranyakashyap called his sister Holika, a she-demon, to kill Prahlad. Holika had been given a boon that fire could not destroy her. She decided to take Prahlad in her lap and sit on a burning pyre.

As the flames engulfed them Prahlad called aloud for Lord Vishnu's help. To everybody's surprise, the fire slowly consumed Holika and she burned to death. Prahlad emerged safe and sound.

## 5 Rama Is Born

King Dasaratha was unhappy because he had no heir to the throne. One day, Sage Vashishtha, asked the king to perform the *Ashvamedha yajna*.

Meanwhile, Ravana, had acquired the boon of immortality from Brahma, and was creating havoc in heaven and on earth. The gods appealed to Vishnu to get rid of him.

While the *yajna* was going on, a magnificent figure arose and gave King Dasaratha a bowl of *payasam*, a rice pudding prepared as an offering to the gods.

The king gave the *payasam* to each of his three wives—Kausalya, Kaikeyi, and Sumitra.

Soon, the queens gave birth to beautiful boys. Lord Rama, the reincarnation of Vishnu, was born to Kausalya; Bharat to Kaikeyi; and Laxmana and Shatrughna to Sumitra.

## 6 Rama and Laxmana

King Dasaratha's children were taught by the great sage Vashishtha. Though all four were very bright, Rama was the best and most adored.

One day, Sage Vishwamitra came to King Dasaratha and told him that two demons named Mareecha and Subahu were troubling the sages. He asked King Dasaratha to send his brave sons, Rama and Laxmana, to fight the two demons and enable the sages to perform their rituals. King Dasaratha sent Rama and Laxmana with the sage to the forest of Dandka.

The brothers kept a strict watch outside the sage's hut while the rituals were going on. Five days passed peacefully but on the morning of the sixth day a thunderous roar was heard. All looked up to see an approaching army of demons clouding the skies. Rama aimed his powerful arrow at Mareecha and hurled him into the sea. The next shot at Subahu killed the monster immediately. The two brothers then easily defeated the rest of the army.

## 7 The Marriage of Shiva and Parvati

The king of the Himalayas, Himavantha and his wife, Menadevi were devotees of Shiva. They wanted a daughter who would grow up to be the wife of Shiva. So Menadevi performed *tapasya* to please Gauridevi, wife of Shiva. She sat and prayed for days on end, without any food and water. Pleased, Gauridevi promised to be born as Menadevi's daughter.

Gauridevi jumped into a fire and died. She was then reborn as Menadevi's daughter and was named Parvati. The first word that she uttered was 'Shiva.' She grew up to be a beautiful woman. Meanwhile, Shiva who was very sad at the death of his wife had started a long meditation. Himavantha was worried that Shiva would not accept Parvati as his wife as he was in deep meditation and requested Narada to solve his problem. Narada told him that Parvati could win Shiva over through prayers. So Himavantha sent Parvati to the place where Shiva was meditating. Day and night Parvati worshipped and served Shiva.

Though pleased with her devotion, Shiva decided to test her. He disguised himself as a young Brahmin and told Parvati that it would not be good for her to marry Shiva who lived like a beggar and had nothing. Parvati got very angry when she heard these words about Shiva. She told him that she would marry no one but Shiva. Pleased with her answer Shiva came back to his real form and agreed to marry Parvati. Himavantha performed the wedding with great splendour.

## 8 Lord Vishnu

Vishnu is the preserver of the universe. Along with Brahma and Shiva he makes up the Holy Trinity.

He is depicted as having four arms and standing on a pink lotus. The first hand holds a conch shell, which indicates the spread of the divine sound 'Om.' One hand holds a discus, which is a reminder of the wheel of time, and to lead a good life; one hand holds a lotus which is an example of glorious existence and the fourth hands holds a mace.

He travels on the swift-flying eagle, Garuda, and is often shown resting on the coiled body of Seshnag in his abode, Kshirasagar. The goddess Laxmi is the consort of Vishnu.

It is believed that Vishnu had ten avatars or forms, the most popular being Rama and Krishna. Vishnu is yet to appear in his tenth incarnation, which is believed to arrive when the world will be on the brink of complete chaos.

## 9 Hanuman

Punjikasthala was the beautiful attendant of the teacher of the gods, Vrihaspati. She once insulted a holy sage and was cursed to change into a female monkey. If she gave birth to an incarnation of Shiva she could be relieved of the curse.

Punjikasthala was reborn as Anjana, the daughter of Rishi Gautam. Anjana was a devotee of Shiva and began praying to him. Pleased with her devotion Shiva promised to be born to her and relieve her of the curse.

During King Dasaratha's *yajna* to beget sons, when the fire god, Agni, appeared with a bowl of *payasam* to be fed to Dasaratha's three wives; just then, an eagle swooped down and flew away with some of it in its beak. It dropped the *payasam* over the spot where Anjana was praying to Shiva. The god of winds, Pavana, blew hard and made the *payasam* fall in her outstretched hands.

Anjana ate the *payasam*. Soon, Shiva, incarnated as a monkey, was born as Hanuman. Pavana became Hanuman's godfather.

Because the wind helped in making this possible, Hanuman is called *Pavanputra* or 'son of the wind.'

With the birth of Hanuman, Anjana was released from the curse. Before she returned to heaven, Hanuman asked his mother about his life ahead. Anjana lovingly assured him that he would never die.

Hanuman grew up and inherited his father's mighty strength and the ability to fly swiftly.

The birth of Hanuman is celebrated as Hanuman Jayanti.

## 10 Balarama Is Born

Kansa had imprisoned his sister, Devaki and Vasudeva and killed every child that was born to Devaki. When Devaki and Vasudeva's sixth child was also killed by the wicked king, Devaki was very upset and began praying to Vishnu for help.

One night, Vishnu appeared in Devaki's dream and said that the divine king of snakes, Seshnaga, would be born as her seventh child. He told her that the child would not be killed by Kansa. Miraculously, a baby that was conceived in Devaki's womb was transferred to the womb of Rohini, Vasudeva's second wife. This baby was Balarama. Balarama was the elder brother of Krishna.

Balarama was born in the village of Gokul in the full moon month of *Sridhara* in July. This is where, his younger brother Krishna, the eighth born, also joined him later.

He was named Rama but came to be known as Balarama, which means 'strong Rama' for his superior strength.

# 11 Birth of Krishna

Kansa had imprisoned Devaki and Vasudeva. Devaki prayed to Vishnu. He promised to be born as her child. Accordingly, Devaki gave birth to her eighth child, the eighth incarnation of Lord Vishnu, on a stormy night on the eighth day of the month of *Shravana*.

Miraculously, the iron chains round Vasudeva opened. The guards fell asleep and a voice said, "Take your child to the safe arms of Nanda in Gokul."

Vasudeva placed the baby in a casket and stealthily crept out of the prison. Amidst heavy rains, Vasudeva crossed the river Yamuna carrying the new-born on his head.

Seshnaga, the king of snakes, placed himself behind Vasudeva and spread his hood covering them like an umbrella. Vasudeva crossed the river safely and reached the gates of Gokul.

# 12 Matsya Avatar

Lord Vishnu once declared that whenever there is any danger on the earth, he would adopt a different form and come down on earth to save its people.

One day, when Brahma was sleeping, Hayagriva, a horse-headed demon, stole the holy Vedas from under Brahma's head. He then ran away and hid in the depths of the ocean. Brahma had to read the holy books to create the universe. Since he was unable to do so now, he was very disturbed and approached Vishnu for help.

Vishnu took the form of a fish and dived into the ocean to get back the Vedas from the terrible demon. There was a fierce fight between Vishnu and Hayagriva, which went on and on. Finally, Vishnu killed the demon and brought the holy books back to Brahma. Brahma was very thankful and was able to resume reading the Vedas.

Vishnu in this fish form is called Matsya Avatar.

## 13 Ganesha

One day Parvati wanted to take a bath, but there was no one to guard her. So she created a young boy, and asked him not to allow anyone to enter while she bathed. She named the little boy, Ganesha. Soon Lord Shiva returned and was surprised to see Ganesha. Ganesha refused to allow Lord Shiva to enter the house since Parvati had asked him not to allow anyone. Lord Shiva was furious and sent his bull, Nandi, to fight the boy but Ganesha defeated Nandi. In a fit of rage, Lord Shiva cut off Ganesha's head.

When Parvati came out and saw her son dead, she was furious. Shiva tried to console her but she couldn't stop crying. She ordered Shiva to bring him back to life. Shiva asked Nandi to bring the head of the first creature he found. Nandi went to obey his command and returned with the head of an elephant. Lord Shiva placed the head of the elephant on Ganesha's body and brought him back to life.

## 14 Sita's Swayamvara

King Janaka of Mithila organized a grand *swayamvara* of his beautiful daughter, Sita. A *swayamvara* was a ritual where kings and princes from far and near would visit the king's court to ask for the princess's hand, but only the bravest would be selected. King Janaka announced that he had a mighty bow, which was blessed by Shiva. The one who could string the bow would marry Sita.

Many princes tried but all failed. Nobody could even move the bow. Rama and Laxmana were also present. All eyes then went to Rama, when his turn came.

Rama easily lifted the bow with one hand and strung it with a thunderous twang. The bow broke into pieces.

Then, Sita walked up to Rama and garlanded him. The wedding was celebrated with great joy.

## 15 Kansa and Putana

Kansa knew that the eighth child, according to the prophecy, would be his slayer. When the eighth child was born to Devaki, Kansa immediately arrived at the prison and snatched the baby from Devaki. This was actually the goddess Yogmaya. She laughed at Kansa for his foolishness and told him that his slayer had been born and was living in Gokul.

Kansa was furious and ordered his men to kill all children born on the same day as Krishna, but the men returned empty-handed. Finally, Kansa sent Putana, the queen of the demons, to kill Krishna. She planned to kill him by feeding him poisoned milk.

Krishna was lying in the cot in the courtyard of Nanda's house. Putana assumed the form of a beautiful maiden and happened to be passing by. When she saw Krishna, she asked for permission to pick him up. She offered her breast to feed him and Krishna sucked the life out from her.

## 16 Foolish Bhasmasura

Bhasmasura was a very powerful *asur* (demon). He was very big and strong but at the same time, he was also very foolish.

Bhasmasura prayed to Shiva. Pleased with his devotion, Shiva decided to grant him a boon. When Shiva asked Bhasmasura what he wanted, Bhasmasura said, "Lord, please grant me the wish that whichever person, place or thing I place my right hand on, is reduced to ashes." Lord Shiva granted him the boon and Bhasmasura was very happy.

Having got the boon, the wicked Bhasmasura tried the boon on Shiva himself. As a result, Shiva started running from Bhasmasura to save himself. Seeing Shiva's plight, Lord Vishnu decided to help him. He changed himself into a beautiful young maiden, called Mohini. When Bhasmasura saw Mohini, he was enchanted by her beauty. He forgot all about Shiva and started to run after Mohini instead. He was attracted by Mohini's beauty and asked her to marry him. Mohini agreed to marry him, but she had a condition. She asked Bhasmasura to touch his head and promise her that he would not marry again if she became his wife. Bhasmasura agreed. As soon as the foolish demon touched his head, he was reduced to ashes. That is how Vishnu succeeded in saving Shiva from Bhasmasura.

# 17 Around the Universe

Lord Shiva and Parvati had four children—Ganesha, Laxmi, Saraswati, and Kartik. Each of them had their own *vahana* or 'vehicle.' Ganesha, the god of wealth and wisdom, had a mouse; Laxmi, the goddess of wealth, had a white owl; Saraswati, the goddess of education, had a swan; and Kartik, the god of war, had a peacock.

One day, Shiva and Parvati were sitting together and Ganesha and Kartik were playing nearby. Shiva decided to test their strength. He declared that of the two, the sibling who first completed circling the universe thrice would be seen as being the mightier one.

Promptly, Kartik sat on his peacock and sped off on his journey around the universe. He travelled over the seas, the mountains, the earth, the moon, and the galaxies. He rushed from one place to another in his effort to beat Ganesha. He knew that with a mouse for a *vahana* and a large potbelly, Ganesha would never be able to compete with him.

Meanwhile, Ganesha sat peacefully at his parents' feet. He quietly got up and walked around his parents thrice. When Kartik came back, he was astonished to see Ganesha happily sitting in Shiva's lap. He could not understand how Ganesha could have returned before he did. Being hot-headed, he accused Ganesha of being unfair. Ganesha said that his parents were his universe and by circling them, he had proved himself.

Shiva was very pleased with Ganesha's wisdom. He declared that before starting any work, people would first pray to Ganesha. This is why it is considered auspicious to worship Ganesha before undertaking any task.

# 18 Krishna's Love for Butter

As Krishna grew older his pranks increased. Tales of his love for milk and butter had spread in every household. Whenever the milkmaids crossed the fields, Krishna and his friends shot pebbles at them to break the milk pitchers.

Knowing Krishna's love for milk products, Yashoda kept the butter jars tied together and hung them from a high ceiling where Krishna's hands could not reach. One day, seeing Krishna fast asleep, she went to fetch a bucket of water from the nearby well. Krishna jumped up and whistled aloud. A group of boys and monkeys came running into their home. They quickly huddled together to help Krishna stand on their shoulders and get down the jars.

Then they sat down to eat the butter. They were so absorbed that they did not see Yashoda enter the house.

Furious, she chased them with a stick. The monkeys and friends escaped but Krishna got a good spanking from his mother!

# 19 Shantanu

Once, King Shantanu of Hastinapur met a woman named Ganga, on the banks of river Ganga. He wanted to marry her and she agreed to do so on the condition that he would never ask her any questions.

Soon, Ganga gave birth to a child but drowned him in the river. Shantanu was shocked. One by one, she drowned six more children. Finally, when she was going to drown her eighth child, Shantanu asked her why she was doing so.

She said that she was the goddess Ganga under a curse to be born as a human. The children were *vasus* (demi-gods) and she was freeing them of the curse. But since Shantanu had stopped her, the eighth child would have to live the life of a human. Saying so, Ganga left.

The eighth child grew up to be the great warrior, Bhishma.

# 20 Trinavarta and Krishna

One day, Yashoda got busy in her household chores and she left baby Krishna in the courtyard all by himself. Just then, Kansa's servant, the demon Trinavarta, appeared in the form of a whirlwind and flew away with the child.

Raising a whirlpool of dust all across the city of Gokul, Trinavarta rocketed higher and higher into the sky. The entire city was covered with a dense cloud of dust, so thick that nobody could see anything.

Yashoda got alarmed and unable to find her baby, wept aloud.

Trinavarta tried to take the baby on his shoulders, but Krishna made himself very heavy. Unable to bear Krishna's growing load, he was forced to come down on the ground.

Krishna became as huge as a mountain and grabbed Trinavarta's neck. The demon tried to get out of the clutches of Krishna. Just then Krishna released him and he fell with a huge thud over Gokul and died.

## 21 Brahma

Brahma is the creator of the universe. He is depicted as sitting on a lotus with four heads and four arms. The hands hold the lotus, a string of beads used to keep track of time, a water pot to create life, and the four Vedas respectively. The four heads represent the sacred knowledge of the four Vedas—Rig, Yajur, Sama, and Atharva Vedas.

His vehicle is the swan, which is known for its ability to judge between good and evil. Brahma is considered to have been self-born from the lotus, which grew in the navel of Vishnu at the beginning of creation.

His companion is Saraswati, who is the goddess of learning and knowledge. She provides Brahma with the necessary knowledge for creating the universe.

## 22 Ganesha's Mouse

Once there was a demon called Gajamugasuran. He was a great devotee of Shiva and pleased with his penance, Shiva granted him some boons. Gajamugasuran became very proud and powerful and he started troubling the gods. Tired of his antics, the gods asked Shiva to save them from Gajamugasaran. Shiva sent Ganesha to help the gods. Ganesha went with several weapons such as bow and arrow, sword, and even an axe to destroy Gajamugasuran. But the demon had been given a boon that none of these weapons could cause him harm, so Ganesha's attempts to destroy the demon proved to be ineffective. Finally, Gajamugasuran took the form of a small mouse and rushed towards Ganesha. Ganseha was very clever and immediately sat on the little mouse. Gajamugasuran was defeated and was forced to apologise for his deeds. Since then, Ganesha is always accompanied by a mouse as his vehicle.

# 23 The Vision

As a child, Krishna was very naughty. He was very fond of butter and would often steal milk and butter from other houses, and the women would come complaining to Yashoda about her son's mischievous activities.

One day, while playing in the fields, little Krishna secretly ate mud. His friends went and told Yashoda about this. When Krishna returned home, Yashoda caught Krishna by his ears and scolded him for putting dirt in his mouth. Krishna promptly replied that he had had a fight with his friends in the morning and to take revenge they were all lying and that Yashoda shouldn't believe them. He said that she was being unfair as she believed them instead of believing her son.

Yashoda knew her son too

well. She ordered, "If you have not taken any mud, then open your mouth. I shall see for myself."

Krishna obediently opened his mouth. But when Yashoda peered into his mouth, she was wonderstruck. She saw the entire universe: the mountains, the oceans, the planets, air, fire, moon and the stars in his small mouth. Yashoda was stunned and began to wonder whether she were dreaming or actually seeing something extraordinary. She fell on the ground, unconscious.

When she recovered, she realised what had happened. The Lord Almighty, in all his glory, was before her very eyes. It was little Krishna, the incarnation of Vishnu. Yashoda took the little boy on her lap and hugged him and cried with joy.

# 24 The Legend of Brahma's Four Heads

Brahma, the creator of the universe, is depicted as having four heads, though originally he had five.

While creating the universe Brahma made a beautiful woman and named her Satarupa. But Brahma was charmed by his own creation. He had never before seen such a fine beauty. To enable himself to see her from all angles he gave himself a second, third, and fourth head. Wherever Satarupa went she found Brahma's eyes staring at her. Disgusted, she rose skywards and in order to see her, Brahma created a fifth head for himself.

Lord Shiva, the destroyer, was watching all this and Brahma's actions greatly angered him. He felt that as Brahma had created Satarupa, she was like his daughter and it was his duty to protect her.

He felt that it was wrong on Brahma's part to be in love with her and to teach him a lesson Shiva struck off Brahma's fifth head.

# 25 Kartikeya

Once upon a time a demon called Taraka performed a long and difficult *tapasya*. Pleased with him, Brahma gave him the boon that only a son of Shiva could kill him.

After getting this powerful boon, Taraka became very proud and selfish and started destroying heaven and earth. Seeing the chaos, the gods were in a fix and requested Shiva to stop Taraka. At that time, Shiva did not have any sons. To create a son, Shiva took a form with six faces. Each face had a third eye. Six sparks came out of these eyes and formed into six babies. Parvati, wife of Shiva, was very happy and took all the babies in her arms to hug them. But she hugged them so tightly that the six babies turned into one baby with six heads.

This baby was called Kartikeya. Kartikeya was a strong boy and went with an army of gods to fight with Taraka and killed him.

Since then, Kartikeya is known as the god of war.

# 26 Lord Buddha

Buddha, meaning 'the enlightened one,' was born in the ancient city of Kapilavastu, to King Sudhodana and Queen Maya. He was an avatar of Vishnu. The young prince, named Siddhartha, was not attracted to the luxurious life of the palace. Instead he became sad seeing misery of the common man.

Seeing his son lose interest in worldly matters, Sudhodana married Siddhartha to a young woman. Though they had a son and Siddhartha continued living in the palace, he remained unhappy.

One day, leaving his family behind, he walked out of the palace to lead a hermit's life in the forests.

Under the bodhi tree in Gaya, he achieved nirvana or eternal peace. He travelled all over India and began spreading his message. Buddhism is the name of the religion that is based on the teachings of Buddha.

## 27 Ganesha Curses the Moon

Ganesha, the pot-bellied elephant god, loved food and could spend an entire day, eating. Once, on a moonlit night after stuffing himself with his favourite sweet, the *ladoo*, he went for a ride on his *vahana*, a tiny rat. The rat could not bear his weight and tripped. Ganesha fell on the ground with a thud and broke a tusk. The moon laughed, seeing this funny sight.

Seeing the moon mocking him, Ganesha got angry. He cursed the moon saying that any man who looked at the moon on Ganesha Chaturthi, the birthday of Ganesha, would be wrongly blamed.

The moon, realised its mistake, and begged Ganesha to remove the curse. But Ganesha was adamant. Finally, after a long time, Ganesha gave in and reduced the punishment. He could not take back his curse but said that the falsely accused man would have to look at the moon on the second day of the fortnight to win back his good name.

## 28 A Meeting with Death

Once there was a boy called Nachiketa. One day, his father performed a *yajna*. He donated cows to the Brahmins. Nachiketa knew it was customary to offer dear things as a sacrifice to the gods. He asked his father, "Whom will you give me to?" Disturbed by his question, his father angrily replied, " I give you to Yama, the god of death."

Nachiketa went to Yama's kingdom. He waited three days without food. When Yama returned, he was pleased with Nachiketa's devotion and granted him three wishes. Nachiketa asked for his father to be pleased with him. For his second wish, Nachiketa asked to go to heaven. Yama agreed. Finally, Nachiketa wanted to know the secret of life and death. Yama hesitated, but looking at his determination he granted his last wish too.

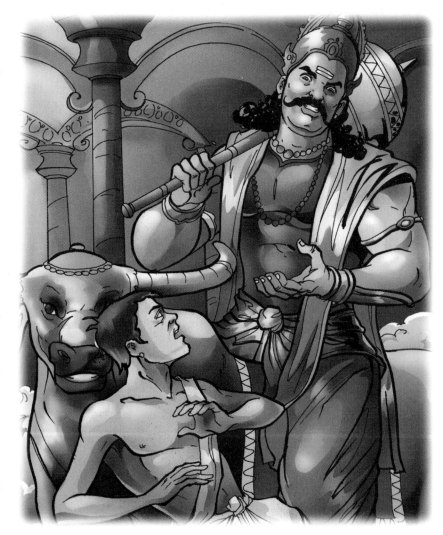

## 29 Krishna and Bakasura

Kansa, the wicked maternal uncle of Krishna, knew that Krishna was in Gokul and feared that one day, Krishna would kill him. Kansa wanted to kill Krishna and spent all his time, thinking of devious plans for doing so. One day, he called the demon Bakasura and asked him to go and kill the infant Krishna. Bakasura, decided to take the form of a huge bird to frighten young Krishna.

One day Krishna was playing with his friends in the forests of Gokul, when he saw a giant bird swooping down on them. Krishna at once understood that this bird was none other than a demon sent by Kansa to kill him.

As the bird came closer, the brave Krishna caught its huge beak and quickly got inside it. Inside the beak, Krishna wriggled around so much that Bakasura's beak was broken. Exhausted, Bakasura died after some time and fell to the ground.

Krishna's friends hugged him in joy.

## 30 Kurma Avatar

Vishnu is known as the great preserver and protector of all forms of life.

Once during *samudra manthan* or the great churning of the seas by the gods and the demons, Vishnu decided to change himself into a tortoise and help in this mammoth task.

This churning was to bring out the potent drink *amrita* from the depths of the ocean to help regain power and immortality.

The huge mountain, Mandara, was used as the pole for churning the water. But as the churning continued, the mountain began descending into the sea.

The worried gods then prayed to Vishnu, who changed himself into a huge tortoise and placed the mountain on his back.

The churning began and this time it continued smoothly.

# 31 The Great Sacrifice

Shibi Rana was a great king. He was famous for his truthfulness, justice, and keeping his word.

One day, the gods decided to test him. Once, the king saw an eagle chasing a dove. The dove was frantically looking for a place to hide and came and settled in the king's lap. The dove said, "O king, please save my life." The king had taken a vow to protect anyone who took his shelter. Shibi Rana hid the dove in his lap. When the eagle saw this, he said, "O king, you have hidden my prey. Please leave the dove and let me satisfy my hunger."

The king wanted to protect the dove but at the same time, he did not want to deprive the eagle of his prey. He offered to give the eagle the same amount of meat in return. The eagle demanded flesh from the king's right thigh on the condition that not a tear should fall from his eye while his thigh is cut. The king thought that cutting away a little flesh from his body would not kill him and the dove would also be saved at the same time, so he agreed. The dove was placed on one side of a balance and the king's flesh on the other. But no matter how much flesh was added, the dove was always heavier. A small tear appeared in the king's left eye. When the eagle confronted him, the king explained that the left eye was sad because no flesh had been taken from the left thigh. At this, the eagle and the dove vanished.

Shibi Rana had passed the test and the gods blessed him.

# Contents

*The Story of the Month: Samudra Manthan*

...er side. As the churning began and the massive waves whirled, an extremely poisonous drink called *halahal* came out. The gods became scared because this blue drink could destroy creation.

They all got together and prayed to the powerful Shiva to help them. Shiva appeared before all and gulped the entire poison. But, he did not swallow it keeping the poison in his throat. Since then,

к.
ara,
ir the
entered
into the
n. To stop
ckly trans-
o a tortoise
placed    the
mountain

Shiva's throat became blue, and he became known as Neelkantha or the blue-throated one.

The churning continued and poured forth a number of gifts and treasures. They included Kamadhenu, the wish-fulfilling cow; the goddess of wealth, Laxmi; the wish-fulfilling tree, Kalpavriksha; and finally, came Dhanvantari carrying the pot of *amrita* and a book of medicine called *Ayurveda*. Once the *amrita* was out, the demons forcefully took it away. Two demons, Rahu and Ketu, disguised themselves as gods and drank the *amrita*. The sun and moon gods recognised it to be a trick    and

complained to Vishnu, who in turn, severed their heads with his *Sudarshan Chakra*. As the divine nectar did not get time to reach below the throat, the heads remained immortal, but the body below died. This helps Rahu and Ketu take revenge on the Sun and Moon by devouring them every year during solar and lunar eclipse.

A great war between the gods and demons followed. Finally, Vishnu disguised as the enchanting Mohini tricked the demons and recovered the nectar.

While fleeing the clutches of the demons, Vishnu gave the *amrita* to his

winged charioteer, Garuda. But the demons caught up and a tussle followed. During this tussle few drops of the drink fell at Ujjain, Nasik, Allahabad, and Haridwar.

The drops are said to have purified the land and it is here that every year devotees come to wash away their sins in the famous assembly called Kumbh Mela.

Once Garuda got back and the gods drank the nectar, they became immortal. But as some demons had managed to taste a few drops of the drink, they too became immortal and to this day the fight between good and evil continues.

# 1 The Two Boons

Once there was a fierce battle between the gods and the demons in the forest of Dandaka. King Dasaratha went to help Indra and was accompanied by Queen Kaikeyi. In the fierce battle with the great demon Shambara, Dasaratha fell to the ground and lost consciousness. Kaikeyi quickly drove the chariot away from the battlefield and thus saved his life. The king was very pleased and grateful and granted her two boons.

Years later, King Dasaratha decided to let his sons take over the reigns of Ayodhya. He wanted to crown Rama as the next king.

Kaikeyi's personal maid, Manthara, was a very sharp and wicked lady. She went to the queen and told her that this decision was unjust and that Kaikeyi's son, Bharata, was more deserving and should be crowned king instead. Kaikeyi said that she was happy because even Rama was like her own child and moreover, Bharata was very loyal to Rama. At this, Manthara retorted that Rama would become very powerful once he became the king and they would all become paupers. She tried to poison Kaikeyi's mind against Rama. She reminded Kaikeyi of Dasaratha's promises and said this was the opportune time for her to reclaim those two wishes.

Kaikeyi was influenced by Manthara's devious plan and under her evil advice, Kaikeyi reminded Dasaratha of his promise. She made Dasaratha crown Bharata king and send Rama into exile for fourteen years.

# 2 Krishna and Kaliya

Once a huge black serpent called Kaliya came to live in the river Yamuna. He poisoned the water of the river with his venom. The people of Vrindavan were very scared of the serpent, who was very strong.

One day, Krishna decided to teach Kaliya a lesson. He jumped into the river to kill the serpent. Kaliya was furious and rushed to attack Krishna. But before the snake could catch him, Krishna quickly climbed on Kaliya's head. To shake him off, Kaliya tried to coil around Krishna and crush him. He even tried to drown him but Krishna stayed underwater without breathing. Eventually, Kaliya got tired. Krishna then started jumping and stamping on Kaliya's head and the serpent started vomiting poison. Krishna continued doing this until Kaliya had spat out all his poison.

Kaliya begged Krishna for forgiveness and Krishna ordered the serpent to leave the Yamuna. Kaliya bowed his head and quietly left, and the people of Vrindavan rejoiced.

# 3 The Story of Devavrata

King Shantanu and goddess Ganga had a son called Devavrata. When Devavrata was just a baby, Ganga had left Shantanu and taken him with her. One day while hunting in the forest, Shantanu was surprised to see that the flow of Ganga had been stopped by a dam built with arrows. He saw a handsome boy carrying a bow and arrow. Suddenly, Ganga came out of the river. She said, "King Shantanu, this is our son, Devavrata. He has been taught the Vedas, the Shastras and weaponry. You may now take him with you."

Shantanu took Devavrata back with him and made him the *yuvraja* (crown prince) of Hastinapur. After a few days, the prince of Shalva attacked Hastinapur but Devavrata bravely fought and defeated him. Shantanu was very proud of his son.

# 4 Bhishma

One day, King Shantanu of Hastinapur went hunting. Suddenly, he smelt a sweet fragrance, which was coming from a beautiful woman named Satyawati.

Shantanu fell in love with Satyawati and asked her fisherman father for permission to marry her. The fisherman agreed on the condition that if Satyawati had a son, he would become the next king. This made Shantanu sad because he already had a son, Devavrata.

Shantanu went back without Satyawati. When Devavrata saw that his father was sad, he went to the fisherman. Devavrata promised him that Satyawati's son would become the next king instead of him. At this the clever fisherman said, "What if your sons try to become king." To satisfy him Devavrata took a *bhishma pratigya* (strict pledge), never to get married and have children. He then took Satyawati to the palace. Because of this strict promise, he became famous as Bhishma.

## 5 Vedavati

King Rathadhwaja broke the family tradition of worshipping goddess Laxmi. Soon, he lost his kingdom. His sons performed a long *tapasya* and prayed to Laxmi to be born in their family. Soon they won their kingdom back. Laxmi was born as a daughter to one of them. When she was born, she was chanting the Vedas (holy verses) and was named Vedavati. When she grew up, she decided to marry Vishnu. She went to a pilgrimage to perform *tapasya*. She was told that she would marry Vishnu in her next birth and continued her *tapasya*.

She was interrupted by Ravana, who wanted her for himself and insulted Vishnu. Vedavati cursed him that in her next birth she would become the cause of his death and then jumped into the fire.

## 6 Vakratunda

Once, Matsar, a demon, asked Sage Shukracharya, "Please tell me how can I rule the worlds?" Shukracharya replied, "You should perform *tapasya* to please Shiva and chant the mantra *Om Namah Shivaya*." Matsar stood on one leg for years, chanting the mantra. Pleased, Shiva bestowed a boon on Matsar that no human, god, or demon could kill him. Matsar took over the three worlds—heaven, earth, and *patal-lok* (the netherworld). He started troubling everyone. Soon, Matsar conquered Kailash, the home of Shiva. The gods, including Shiva, prayed to Ganesha because only his Vakratunda (twisted trunk) form could defeat Matsar. Finally, Ganesha took his Vakratunda form. He used a weapon that entangled Matsar and he prayed to Vakratunda for forgiveness. Vakratunda said, "I will forgive if you promise to return heaven and earth and never trouble anyone." Matsar promised and Vakratunda set him free.

## 7 The Three Princesses

King Shantanu of Hastinapur and his wife Satyawati had two sons, Chitrangada and Vichitravirya. Bhishma, another son of Shantanu, was their guardian. When King Shantanu died Chitrangada was made the king, but when he too died in a battle, Vichitravirya became the king.

One day, Satyawati asked Bhishma to find brides for Vichitravirya. Bhishma went to the court of the king of Kashi where he was holding a *swayamvara* for his three daughters. When the other princes saw Bhishma, they joked that an old man like him had come to marry the young princesses. At this, Bhishma got angry. He forcefully brought the three princesses to Hastinapur. But the first princess, Amba, said that she wanted to marry Prince Shalva. So Bhishma sent her

to him. Ambika and Ambalika were married to Vichitravirya.

One day, Ambika and Ambalika went with their maid to visit Saint Vyasa, who was very ugly. When Ambika saw his face she closed her eyes. So Vyasa cursed her saying she would give birth to a blind son. When Ambalika saw him, she turned pale. Vyasa said that a pale and weak son would be born to her. When the maid saw Vyasa, she was fearless, so Vyasa blessed

her saying that a very intelligent son would be born to her.

As time passed, Ambika gave birth to Prince Dhritarashtra, who was strong but blind. Ambalika gave birth to Pandu who was a great shooter but weak. Though Dhritarashtra was elder, he was not made the king, as he was blind. Instead Pandu became the king. The maid's son Vidura was very wise and was made a minister in the court.

## 8 Kacha and Devyani

The gods and demons were always fighting. But every time the demons were killed, their guru, Shukracharya, would bring them back to life by the secret of *mritasanjibani*. The gods also wanted to learn the secret so they sent Kacha, the handsome son of their guru, Brihaspati, to Shukracharya's ashram.

Kacha fell in love with Devyani, Shukracharya's daughter. When the demons found out that the gods had sent Kacha, they killed him. They mixed his

remains with the wine that Shukracharya drank. When Devyani came to know that Kacha was dead, she begged her father to bring him back to life. But if Shukracharya brought Kacha out of his stomach, he himself would die. So he taught Kacha the secret of *mritasanjibani*.

Shukracharya brought Kacha back to life and he died. Then, Kacha brought Shukracharya back to life. In this way, the lives of both were saved.

Kacha went back to heaven and taught the secret of *mritasanjibani* to the gods.

### 9 Kaikeyi's Resolve

Kaikeyi wanted her son, Bharata, to rule Ayodhya.

She went to King Dasaratha and reminded him of the two boons that he had once granted her for saving his life. Dasaratha asked her what she wanted. She asked the king to grant her wishes that Bharata be crowned king of Ayodhya and that Rama be banished to the forest for fourteen years. The king was shocked when he heard this. He had not imagined that Kaikeyi who loved Rama so dearly, could be so cruel.

A heartbroken Dasaratha then pleaded with Kaikeyi and asked her as to how could she be so stubborn and see her son undergo the hardships of banishment. But Kaikeyi would not listen. She reminded Dasaratha that it was wrong on a king's part to break his promises.

Thus, Kaikeyi became the sole cause for Rama's fourteen-year exile to the forests.

### 10 The Goddess Durga

The buffalo demon, Mahisha, performed *tapasya* and for his efforts he received a boon from Brahma that no man or god would be able to kill him. Full of power, he attacked the gods and captured heaven. The gods had to come down and wander about on earth. They were very angry at their condition and their faces began to glow. The light took the shape of a goddess, Durga. Each of the gods gave her a weapon. Himalaya gave her a lion. Riding the lion she began to roar. Mahisha came out of his palace on hearing the roar. Durga killed his army of demons. Mahisha took many forms, but she defeated all of them. Finally, he took the form of a buffalo and attacked her. Durga killed Mahisha with her *trishula*, and today she is worshipped as goddess Durga.

# 11 Goddess Laxmi

Laxmi is the goddess of wealth, beauty, and prosperity.

Golden in complexion, the goddess has four hands and sits on a pink lotus. Holding a lotus bud in each of the two upper hands, she extends her blessings with the other lower ones.

Laxmi is derived from the word 'lakshya,' meaning aim. Her four hands represent the aims of human life. These are *dharma* or righteousness, *kama* or desire, *artha* or wealth and *moksha,* which means freedom from the cycle of birth and death.

Laxmi's vehicle is the nocturnal bird, the owl. Two elephants are also shown standing next to the goddess and spraying water.

Laxmi is Vishnu's wife. The goddess is also called Shri, and is often referred to as the female energy of Vishnu. Laxmi and Vishnu's son is Kama, the god of love and desire.

# 12 Yashoda Ties Krishna

One day, finding young Krishna stealing butter from the kitchen, Yashoda quietly crept up from behind and tried to catch him.

Krishna darted away. Yashoda got a long rope to tie him to a tree and chased after him only to realize that it was impossible for her to catch the quick-footed child. After tiring his mother out, Krishna decided to let his mother tie him up. But Yashoda realised that the rope was too small. Getting some more rope she tied him to the mortar.

Soon there was a loud noise. Everyone rushed out to see that Krishna had dragged the heavy mortar, and when he got stuck between two trees he had pulled so hard that they had fallen down. These trees were the cursed sons of Kuber, the god of wealth. By making them fall Krishna freed them from the curse.

## 13 How Hanuman Got His Name

Hanuman's mother Anjana had told him that all ripe fruits would form his food. One day, when young Hanuman saw the bright yellow sun he thought it to be a ripe fruit and wanted to eat it. He leaped after the sun and put it in his mouth.

When Indra saw Hanuman gobbling the sun, he became anxious. Without the sun, the universe would cease to function.

He soon hurled the *vajra* or thunderbolt and injured the flying Hanuman on his cheek. Hanuman fell unconscious. His father, Vayu, the wind god, became very angry at Indra's act and withdrew himself from the universe.

Once the wind was gone, all living creatures withered and began losing their life. To pacify Vayu, Indra lifted his thunderbolt and Hanuman recovered.

From then on, he became known as Hanuman since *hanu* in Sanskrit means 'cheek.'

## 14 The Fruit Vendor

One day, young Krishna heard a fruit vendor call out, "Who will buy my fresh fruits?"

Seeing the cart full of ripe fruits he ran inside to get grains. Now, in those days all goods used to be bought not with money, but by bartering or exchanging with other items, and Krishna had seen his parents doing that.

Barely managing to hold the grains in his tiny hands Krishna offered him whatever he could. The vendor liked the innocence of the child. He accepted the grains and lovingly filled the child's hands with fruits in return. As he turned to go he found his cart full of precious jewels instead of fruits.

He immediately understood that God had showered blessings for his kindness.

## 15 How Sage Agastya Was Born

Once Indra, the king of gods, asked Agni, the fire god, and Vayu, the wind god, to go and kill all the demons. Agni and Vayu were very powerful and killed most of the demons but the rest hid in the ocean. So they returned and told Indra that they could not kill the rest of the demons.

Indra was very angry. He ordered Agni and Vayu "Even if you have to churn the ocean, you must get those demons out and kill them."

Agni and Vayu said that they didn't want to churn the ocean as there were other creatures living in it and they would also have to suffer because of the demons.

Indra was not convinced and said, "The ocean has given shelter to the wicked and should suffer for that. But you two are trying to evade your duty by disobeying me. I curse you to be born as humans on earth." Thereafter, Agni was born as Sage Agastya while Vayu took birth as Sage Vashishtha.

## 16 The Birth of the Pandavas and Kauravas

Bhishma wanted Pandu, the king of Hastinapur, to get married. Kunti, the adopted daughter of King Kuntibhoja, chose Pandu as her husband and was married to him. Princess Madri of Madra kingdom also wanted to marry Pandu, so she became his second wife.

Gandhari, the princess of Gandhara kingdom, was chosen as the bride for Dhritarashtra. Dhritarashtra was blind, and Gandhari did not want to be better than her husband in any respect. So she tied a silk bandage on her eyes and pledged never to remove it. A suitable bride was also chosen for Vidura, the minister of Hastinapur, who was raised as a brother of Pandu and Dhritarashtra.

As time passed, Kunti gave birth to three sons—Yudhishthira, Bhima, and Arjuna. Madri gave birth to twins and named them Nakula and Sahadeva. As these five were the sons of Pandu, they were called the Pandavas.

Gandhari wanted a hundred children so she prayed to Saint Vyasa who granted her the boon. But Gandhari gave birth to a lump of flesh. Vyasa cut this lump into hundred and one pieces, which formed hundred boys and one girl. These children of Dhritrashtra were called the Kauravas as they belonged to the Kuru dynasty. The eldest of the Kaurava brothers was called Duryodhana.

# 17 Yama Kumar

Once Yama, the god of death, married a woman of earth and started living there. They had a son called Yama Kumar. Yama soon realised that his wife was very cunning. She always quarrelled with him, so he went back to his kingdom. His wife did not teach Yama Kumar anything so when he grew up he was not able to earn his living.

One night, Yama appeared before his son and said that he should learn about medicine. Soon Yama Kumar became a doctor. Yama said, "Every time you see me near a patient, you will know that the patient is going to die. You must refuse to treat that patient." So, Yama Kumar treated only the patients who were going to survive. He became very famous.

One day the princess fell ill.

Many doctors came from far and wide and tried to cure her, but failed. When Yama Kumar went to see her, he found his father there and realised that the princess was going to die. He pleaded and said, "Father, please do not take the princess, she is so young and beautiful." Yama replied, " I have to fulfil my duty, but for your sake I will take her after three days."

Yama Kumar made a plan to save the princess. When Yama returned, he shouted, "Mother! Father is here, you can meet him." Yama did not want to meet his wife, and on hearing this he was so scared that he ran away without taking the princess.

Yama Kumar saved the princess's life. The king was so happy that he got his daughter married to Yama Kumar.

# 18 Sati

Daksha, Brahma's son, had a beautiful daughter named Sati who loved Shiva and wanted to marry him. Daksha considered himself to be greater than Shiva and forbade her. But Shiva and Sati married without his consent.

One day, at a ceremony, Shiva did not stand up to pay his respects to Daksha. Insulted, Daksha vowed to take revenge.

Daksha arranged for a *yajna* and invited all the gods except Shiva. Sati was very hurt and went to meet her father at the ceremony. Daksha insulted Shiva in front of everyone. Unable to bear this, Sati threw herself into the sacrificial fire and died.

This enraged Shiva and he began performing the *tandav* or the dance of destruction, to destroy the entire universe. Brahma appeared and begged Shiva for forgiveness. Shiva relented but cursed Daksha that he would bear a goat's head forever.

Sati was later reborn as Parvati.

# 19 Krishna and the Gopis

Krishna and Balarama were very naughty children. Krishna loved playing the flute while Balarama tended the cows. The young milkmaids called *gopis* liked the sound of the flute and also went along with Krishna and Balarama when they went to graze the cows.

One day, the *gopis* went for a bath in the river nearby. Krishna and his friends decided to play a trick on them. They quietly followed the *gopis* to the river and hid behind the trees.

When the *gopis* shed their clothes and went into the river to bathe, Krishna and his friends emerged from the bushes and took their clothes and hid them. The *gopis* begged and pleaded for their clothes. After teasing them for some time, Krishna finally decided to give back their clothes.

# 20 The Dutiful Son

As the news of Rama's exile spread, sadness descended over the palace and the city of Ayodhya. The people of Ayodhya were heartbroken.

When Rama heard the news, he rushed to meet King Dasaratha and Kaikeyi. Rama saw his father sitting in a corner, tired and defeated. He realised that the only way to solve the problem was to accept Kaikeyi's demands and leave Ayodhya, because that would save not just his but also King Dasaratha's honour and pride.

Rama explained to his father that Bharata was more capable than him and therefore, deserved to be made the king. He said that he wanted to lead a spiritual life and a luxurious life in the palace would come between him and his wish to be with God. Finally, Rama said that he was duty-bound to fulfil his parents' wishes and did not want to hurt them.

Rama touched his parents' feet to take their blessing and quietly left the room.

## 21 Varaha Avatar

Long ago, there lived a demon called Hiranyaksha. He was Hiranyakashyap's brother and was gifted the boon of immortality by Brahma. No god, demon, beast or man could ever kill him.

Hiranyaksha's powers grew by the day. One day, Hiranyaksha snatched the earth and took it with him under the ocean. The gods were alarmed and rushed to Vishnu for help. Vishnu remembered that Brahma had forgotten to grant Hiranyaksha immortality against *varaha*, the two-tusked wild boar. Vishnu changed himself into a *varaha* and dived into the ocean. Seeing Hiranyaksha there he challenged him to a fight. Soon, Vishnu beheaded Hiranyaksha and brought back the earth from the depths of the ocean.

## 22 Rantideva Attains Moksha

Once Brahma and the other gods asked Vishnu, who his most devoted follower was. Vishnu named King Rantideva as his most devout devotee. He had given up his kingdom and had been chanting Vishnu's name while fasting for forty-eight days. Rantideva believed Vishnu lived in all human beings. The gods decided to test Rantideva by seeing if he would share his food after his long fast. Just as Rantideva was about to eat his meal, a Brahmin appeared and begged him for food. Rantideva gave him half his share. The Brahmin blessed him and went away.

In this way, all the gods changed their form and begged Rantideva for food, and he gladly gave them his share. Yama tested him by appearing as an untouchable who needed water. Rantideva willingly gave him water. The gods were very happy. Vishnu appeared and blessed Rantideva and granted him *moksha* which means freedom from all worldly troubles.

# 23 The Story of Sunday

There was once an old woman who worshipped the sun god. Every morning, she would clean her house by plastering it with cow dung. Only then would she cook and eat anything.

She used to collect the cow dung from her neighbour's house. The neighbour's wife did not like this, so one day she tied the cow inside the house. The next day, the old woman did not get any cow dung and could not plaster her house. As the house was not clean, she had to fast that day.

That night, the sun god came in her dream. He promised to give her a cow. The next morning she found a cow and a calf in her house. The neighbour's wife saw this and became jealous. She also saw that the cow produced dung made of gold. She was very greedy and replaced the gold dung with ordinary dung. The sun god saw this and created a storm, so the old woman tied her cow inside the house and found the gold dung.

The neighbour's wife went to tell the king about the magic cow. The king took away the magic cow and plastered his palace with the gold dung. At night the sun god appeared in the king's dream and said that the cow was a gift for the old lady.

When the king woke up, he found that his palace was smelling because the gold dung had turned into ordinary dung. He felt sorry for his actions and returned the cow to the old lady. He punished the neighbour's cunning wife.

He also declared that the people of his kingdom should fast on Sundays, the day of the sun god.

# 24 Brahma Tests Krishna

Brahma was amazed to see little Krishna perform wonderful feats. He thought of a plan to test him.

One day, while Krishna was out with his friends tending the cattle, he found them all disappearing one by one. Seeing the field getting empty this way, Krishna was surprised. He immediately understood that this was the doing of Lord Brahma. But he did not want to return without his friends and cattle as it would make their parents anxious. To convince Brahma of his ability, Krishna started expanding into various forms. As he was god himself, Krishna could take on any form he desired. In a while the entire field was again crowded with all his friends. The calves too appeared, some mooing and some grazing the fields. It looked exactly the same as before.

Brahma was startled. He realised Krishna's immense powers and showered flowers from the heavens above.

## 25 Rama Leaves Ayodhya

Wearing garments of bark and grass, Rama, Laxmana and Sita left Ayodhya. The people of Ayodhya, ran behind the chariot. King Dasaratha also followed, but soon lost consciousness. When Rama reached the banks of the river Tamasa, they halted for the night. The people soon fell asleep. Rama pleaded with Sumantra, the charioteer, to take them away before the people woke up. They continued their journey till they reached the river Ganga. Here they came across the tribal leader Guha, who offered them his hospitality. Rama politely replied that they could not accept these comforts as they were to lead austere lives. Rama asked Sumantra to return to Ayodhya. Sumantra begged to follow his master, but Rama insisted that he should go back and look after the grief-stricken Dasaratha.

Guha ferried Rama, Laxmana and Sita across the Ganga. Sumantra returned to Ayodhya and found that the heartbroken king had died.

## 26 Rama's Exile

Rama gladly accepted the news of his banishment and went to meet his mother Kausalya. Seeing her son she cried out loud, "How can you bear the hardships of living in a forest for fourteen long years?" Rama smiled and assured her that fourteen years would pass very quickly.

As Rama began preparing for his departure, Sita came to him. She begged Rama to take her with him but he refused. Sita replied, "My Lord, not being with you for fourteen years will be a greater hardship. My duty is to be by your side always."

Like Sita, Laxmana too decided to follow the footsteps of his brother. "How can I leave my dear brother to face the dangers all by himself?" he argued.

Seeing Sita and Laxmana's determination, Rama had no choice but to agree to their wish.

## 27 Sage Dadhyan

Fearing an attack from the demons, Indra went to Sage Dadhyan to seek his help and learn the lesson of *Madhu Vidya* or 'honey doctrine,' which erases all fears.

Dadhyan agreed to impart the knowledge to Indra. Indra then warned him, "If you teach this lesson to anybody else, I will cut off your head." The newly gained knowledge lit up Indra's face. Seeing this glow, the twin 'Ashvinis' or godlike creatures wanted to learn *Madhu Vidya*. They went to the sage, but he told them about his promise.

The Ashvinis decided that if they replaced Dadhyan's head with a horse's, they could get the knowledge from the horse's mouth and thus fool Indra. As planned, Dadhyan, with the head of a horse, began teaching.

When Indra heard this, he struck off the horse's head from Dadhyan's body. After he left, the Ashivinis got the original head and attached it to Dadhyan's body.

## 28 Vikram and Betal

King Vikramaditya was a great ruler. Each day, a man brought a fruit as a gift for him. One day Vikram dropped the fruit and a diamond fell out. Vikram thanked the man and asked him, what he wanted in return. He asked Vikram to bring Betal, a ghost hanging from a tree in the graveyard.

Brave Vikram went to the graveyard and pulled Betal down on to his shoulder. As he started walking back, Betal said, "I will tell you a story and then ask a question. You must tell me the answer otherwise I will break your head. But if you speak I will fly back to the tree." Vikram agreed

This was the start of a series of stories Betal told Vikram, but each time Betal asked Vikram a question, Vikram answered and clever Betal flew back to the tree.

# Contents

*The Story of the Month:   Brave Dhruva*

The Story of the Month
# Brave Dhruva

# Brave Dhruva

King Uttanpada had two wives. His first wife, Suniti, was the daughter of a tribal chief. His second wife, Suruchi, was the daughter of a rich king. Suniti had a son named Dhruva and Suruchi's son was named Uttam. Dhruva was the elder of the two, so it was his right to become the next king.

But Suruchi was very selfish; she hated her stepson Dhruva and wanted her son Uttam to be the ruler. Uttanpada loved Suruchi more than Suniti because she was beautiful. Under her influence, he ordered Suniti and Dhruva to leave the palace.

Mother and son started living in a small hut near the forest. Suniti told Dhruva stories about God and Dhruva always thought about God.

One day, Dhruva went to the palace and saw Uttam sitting on his father's lap. But when Dhruva tried to do the same, Suruchi stopped him and said, "There is no place for you on your father's lap. Only my son can sit on his lap." Dhruva looked at his father hoping that he would stop Suruchi and take him on his lap. But his father did not say anything and ignored him.

Deeply hurt, Dhruva

returned to his mother. Weeping bitterly he asked her why he had no place on his father's lap and why they had no place in the palace. Suniti had no answer to her son's questions. Dhruva said, "You told me that God is good, he helps those who pray to him. I will go and find God, he will certainly give me my place." Dhruva decided to go to the forest and pray until God appeared before him. In the forest, he met Narada Muni, who was worried that a five-year-old boy like him would face many difficulties in the forest. He warned Dhruva that wild animals could eat him up. But Dhruva was determined to find Lord Vishnu. Impressed by his

determination, Narada taught him how to survive in the forest. He also taught him the mantra *'Om Namo Bhagavathe Vasudevaya'* by chanting which he could please Lord Vishnu.

For many months, Dhruva prayed in the forest, and faced many difficulties. He even stopped eating. With every breath, he chanted the mantra in praise of God. Finally, Lord Vishnu was pleased with his determination and appeared before him. He not only granted Dhruva a place on his father's lap, but also a permanent place in the sky after his death.

When Uttanpada heard that his son was living in the forest, he was sorry for his actions. Narada Muni told him that his son had performed difficult prayers in the forest and was blessed by Lord Vishnu himself. When Dhruva returned, Uttanpada was waiting for him at the gates of his kingdom. He took his son lovingly into his arms. He brought him and Suniti back to the palace. Uttanpada immediately made Dhruva the king, saying that the boy who could face such difficulties at such a young age,

could easily rule the kingdom. Uttanpada himself went to live in an ashram.

Dhruva became a wise king and ruled for many years. He spread the message of peace and justice in his kingdom. When he died, he became a star in the sky. This star, called the Pole Star or Dhruva Tara is still seen shining in the sky. It is the only star that has a permanent place and does not change its position in the sky. All the other stars and constellations move around it throughout the year. Travellers look up to the Dhruva Tara in the night to find their way.

# 1  The Enlightened Butcher

Kaushika, a young man, wanted to go off to a hermitage to study the Vedas.

His old parents requested him to stay back and look after them. But Kaushika left his parents and went away. In due course he mastered the Vedas and became a saint.

One day, some bird droppings fell on him. Furious, Kaushika shot a fiery gaze and burnt the bird to ashes.

Then he went out asking for alms. A lady busy with her chores asked him to wait. Kaushika felt insulted and cursed her. She replied that a saint should control his anger and not kill animals. She also suggested that he meet the holy Dharmavyadha in Mathura and learn about virtue.

Kaushika rushed to Mathura, but when he reached there he found Dharmavyadha running a butcher shop. He wondered how a holy man could butcher animals. Dharmavyadha reminded him of the bird he killed and added that he was merely doing his duty of carrying on the family trade. He said that a farmer who tills the land also tramples insects unknowingly.

After that Dharmavyadha introduced his family. He said it gave him great pleasure to serve his parents and fulfil the duties of a father.

Kaushika realised his mistake and felt ashamed that he had ignored his duty. He understood that the true virtue of man lies in carrying out one's *dharma* or task.

He thanked Dharmavydha and rushed back to his old parents. His parents were delighted to have him back.

# 2  A Mountain on a Finger

The people of Vrindavan worshipped Indra, the god of rain. Indra was very proud and arrogant and so Krishna decided to teach him a lesson. One day, he told the people that instead of worshipping Indra, they should worship the Govardhan Mountain and its forests on which their livelihood depended.

The people of Vrindavan obeyed Krishna and stopped worshipping Indra. Indra became angry and decided to punish them. He called upon the clouds, which were under his control and asked them to rain continuously over Vrindavan. The people were terrified by the heavy rains and thought that the flood would destroy their village and they would all die. Krishna lifted the Govardhan entire mountain on the little finger of his left hand. He held the mountain like an umbrella for seven days and seven nights over the people of Vrindavan.

At last, Indra realised his mistake and was ashamed. He asked the clouds to stop raining and apologised to Krishna.

## 3 Krishna and Akrura

Stories about Krishna's deeds spread far and wide. Hearing them, Kansa came to believe that Krishna was the eighth child of Devaki who would slay him. He wanted to kill Krishna. One day, Narada Muni came to Kansa and revealed Krishna and Balaram's whereabouts. Kansa thought of a plan to bring Krishna to Mathura.

Kansa called his minister, Akrura, and sent him as a messenger to invite Krishna to a holy *yajna* in Mathura.

Unfortunately, Kansa did not know that Akrura was a great devotee of Krishna. When Akrura reached Gokul, he was filled with joy and fell at Krishna's feet. Akrura began crying and he told Krishna of Kansa's cruel plan.

Krishna laughed at Kansa's foolishness and decided to go to Mathura.

## 4 The Merchant's Son

There was a rich merchant who longed for a son. He prayed to Shiva who blessed him with a son but said that he would live only for twelve years. The merchant started praying and fasting with more devotion.

When his son was eleven years old, he sent him to Kashi for spiritual education. On the way, the boy stopped at the capital where the princess was getting married. The groom's father wanted to hide the fact that his son was one-eyed and asked the merchant's son to pose as the groom. After the wedding, the merchant's son wrote the truth on a scarf. He gave it to the princess and went to Kashi. When the princess read the scarf, she refused to accept the one-eyed groom and waited for the merchant's son.

When the merchant's son completed twelve years, he died. But Shiva was pleased with the merchant's devotion and brought his son back to life. His son returned bringing the princess as his wife.

# 5 The Pandavas

The Pandavas were the princes of Hastinapur. The reason they were so called was because they were the sons of Pandu, the king of Hastinapur. The first three Pandavas—Yudhishthira, Bhima, and Arjuna—were the sons of Pandu's first wife, Kunti, and the youngest Pandavas— Nakula and Sahadeva—were the sons of Madri, Pandu's second wife. King Pandu and Madri had died, so Kunti brought them up. All the five brothers had great qualities. They were brave and intelligent. They had learnt many arts and mastered weaponry. Yudhisthira, the eldest, was known for his truthfulness and principles. Bhima was very strong and fond of eating. Arjuna was a great archer and was a favourite with his elders. There was a lot of love and brotherhood among them.

# 6 How the Moon Lost Its Light

King Daksha Prajapati had twenty-seven daughters. All of them were married to Chandra, the moon god, on the condition that he would treat them equally. Chandra visited the palace of one wife each night. But he loved only one of his wives, Rohini, and shone the brightest on the night when he visited her. The other wives were very sad and complained about this to their father, who cursed Chandra that he would stop shining.

All day Surya, the sun god, nourished Chandra with his light. And at night Chandra produced the divine drink *soma* which nourished the gods. But due to Daksha's curse on Chandra, the gods lost their source of strength. They ran to Brahma for help. On Brahma's advice, Chandra chanted the 'Mrityunjaya' mantra ten crore times. This pleased Lord Shiva and he partially freed him from the curse. Since then Chandra shines only on certain nights.

## 7 The Proud Gods

The demons once defeated the gods and started ruling the world. They caused a lot of destruction. The gods went to the all-powerful Brahma, the creator of the universe. Brahma blessed them and asked them to fight the demons again. This time the gods won and got their king-dom back.

The gods started celebrating their victory and forgot their duties. They became very proud forgetting that they had won because of Brahma's blessings. Brahma decided to teach them a lesson and sent a *yaksha* (demi-god) to their kingdom.

When Indra, the king of gods, saw the *yaksha*, he sent Agni, the god of fire, to him. Agni said, " I am the powerful god who can burn anything." The *yaksha* gave him a blade of grass and asked him, "Can you burn this?" Agni laughed and said, "This is such a small thing, I can burn it in a second." Agni tried to burn the blade but failed. Ashamed, Agni returned.

Then Indra sent Pawan, the god of wind. Pawan told him that he was a powerful god who could blow away any-thing. The *yaksha* gave him the same blade of grass and asked him, "Can you blow this away?" He placed the blade on his palm and blew at it, but couldn't even move it. He also returned in shame.

Indra then went himself. The *yaksha* said, "You gods have become so proud that you do not recognise that I am Brahma's messenger. I have come to make you realise that it is Brahma who is the most powerful and who made you win. Now leave your pride and fulfil your duties."

## 8 Parshurama

Parshurama, the sixth avatar of Vishnu, had a violent temper. When he heard of Rama break-ing the bow at Sita's *swayam-vara*, he became furious.

Parshurama, a master archer himself and a disciple of Shiva, could not bear to hear of Rama's victory. Besides being a proud Brahmin priest, he dis-liked the idea of a 'Kshatriya,' a man belonging to the warrior class, winning the challenge. He decided to meet Rama and challenge him. On his way to Ayodhya, accompanied by Dasaratha, Laxmana and Sita, Rama met Parshurama. Wield-ing his famous axe, Parshurama promptly attacked Rama. Rama, on the other hand, coun-tered it with his *kondanda* bow, and a fierce battle followed.

While the combat contin-ued, their eyes met and every-thing changed. There was love in place of rage, and respect in-stead of hatred. Recognising each other as different forms of the same supreme Vishnu, they threw their weapons and embraced each other.

# 9 The Devoted Student

Sage Dhoumya lived in his ashram or hermitage in the forest. He had three students—Aruni, Upamanyu, and Ved. Aruni lived in the ashram.

One day Aruni was returning to the ashram after collecting firewood from the forest. It was a cold and windy day. It was raining heavily and the fields were full of water. While he was crossing the field, Aruni saw that at the far end, a barrier of earth had been built to stop water from entering the fields and destroying the crops. But to his dismay, there was a gap in the barrier and water was leaking through it.

Aruni realised that if the leakage was not stopped immediately, the water would enter the fields and destroy the crops. He decided to rush to the ashram, leave the firewood there, and then come back to sort out this problem. Aruni came back and tried to put some mud and straw in the gap. But the pressure of the water was very strong and washed away the mud.

Meanwhile, in the ashram, Sage Dhoumya was worried that it was getting dark and Aruni had not returned. At night, along with the other students, he set out to look for Aruni. As Sage Dhoumya called out Aruni's name, he heard a faint reply. They reached the spot and found Aruni lying on the mound of earth to stop the water from leaking. He was shivering with cold. His teacher was very happy to see his act of devotion. Sage Dhoumya took Aruni back to the ashram and made him warm and comfortable. He declared that he would be famous for his act of devotion.

# 10 Viradha and Rama

As Rama together with Sita and Laxmana roamed the huge Dandaka forest, they chanced upon a man-eating monster called Viradha.

The monster lifted Sita and was about to take her away with him when Rama used his bow. Viradha laughed seeing the puny bow and broke it with his finger.

Realising the futility of using bows to fight with Viradha, Rama and Laxmana decided to tear off his arms. With great gusto they wrenched off Viradha's arms and threw him on the ground. Rama immediately planted his foot on Viradha. The touch had a wondrous effect. Viradha's eyes softened, and with folded hands he said, "Your touch has purified my mind. I am a *gandharva* (nature spirit), and not a monster. Please kill me and relieve me of the curse."

Rama accepted Viradha's request and killed him.

The monster's body changed into a *gandharva* and soared up to the skies.

# 11 The Kauravas

The Kauravas were princes of Hastinapur and the sons of Gandhari and Dhritarashtra. Dhritrashtra and Pandu were brothers. Pandu, even though he was younger, was made king because Dhritarashtra was blind. But after his death, Dhritarashtra became the king of Hastinapur.

Gandhari wanted a hundred sons, and pleased with her, Sage Vyasa granted her a boon that her wish would be fulfilled. But she gave birth to a lump of flesh. Sage Vyasa cut this lump into a hundred and one pieces, and they developed into a hundred boys and one girl. They were called the Kauravas. The eldest was Duryodhana and the second brother was Dusshasan. The Kauravas were jealous of the Pandavas, the sons of Pandu, and were always fighting with them.

# 12 Bharata Returns to Ayodhya

Returning to Ayodhya, Bharata and Shatrughana stopped at the gates of the city.

There was no light, no music or anyone to greet them. The city looked lifeless. Fearing some misfortune had fallen, they rushed towards the palace.

Bharata entered King Dasaratha's chamber, but found it empty. Anxious, he ran to Kaikeyi's room. Seeing her, he exclaimed in joy and enquired about his father and brother Rama's whereabouts.

Kaikeyi avoided his questions, but seeing him grow restless, she told him that Dasaratha was dead and Rama was in exile. Now Bharata would be king.

When Bharata came to know the entire story, he became very angry. He told Kaikeyi that Rama was the rightful king. Bharata fell at Kausalya's feet crying and asked forgiveness for his mother's deceit.

Bharata then performed his father's last rites and made preparations to get Rama back.

# 13 Gajendra

Gajendra was the king of elephants. He lived with his family on a mountain.

On a hot summer day as temperatures soared, he and his family descended the mountain to bathe in the cold waters of the lake below.

Gajendra became playful and began spraying the chilly water with his trunk. A crocodile lived in that lake. As the still waters moved, the crocodile got disturbed. Angry, he stealthily attacked Gajendra and sunk his teeth into his leg. Startled, Gajendra cried out in pain. As his leg bled, he tried to pull it out from the crocodile's jaws. Deeply bruised, his strength failed him. Anxious Gajendra began praying to Vishnu.

In a while, the majestic figure of the lord seated on Garuda emerged. Though crying in pain, Gajendra welcomed Vishnu with a lotus. Vishnu jumped into the lake and swam out to the crocodile. Then tearing its jaws apart he killed the animal and saved Gajendra.

# 14 Poison Kills Poison

Duryodhan, the eldest Kaurava wanted to be king of Hastinapur when he grew up. He always looked for ways to harm his cousins, the Pandavas, who had equal rights to the throne. One day, with the help of his uncle Shakuni, he made a devious plan to kill Bhima, the strongest of the Pandavas. He invited the Pandavas to a picnic near the bank of river Ganga. He had poisoned some of the *laddoos* that were served. He offered these to Bhima who loved food. As soon as Bhima ate them, he fainted under the effect of the poison and Duryodhan pushed him into the river. In the river many poisonous snakes bit Bhima. It is said that 'poison kills poison.' The poison from the snakes cancelled the effect of the poison from the *laddoos*. Bhima was saved; he swam to the surface and returned home.

## 15 Brahma's Lesson

Brahma's creation—the gods, demons, and men—were forever fighting. Their aim was to take control of the entire creation. There was widespread chaos and famine in the three worlds every time they fought.

Brahma grew worried and decided to warn them. One day he boomed, *'da.'* As the loud voice echoed throughout the universe, everyone ran to Brahma for help.

Brahma then asked what the sound meant to each of them.

The gods said 'da' sounded like the word 'damyata,' meaning self-control.

The men said it meant 'dana,' that is, to be giving.

The demons said the voice suggested 'dayadhvam' or merciful.

Brahma then told all that if each were to follow the three principles of 'self-control,' 'charity,' and 'mercy,' he would be happy.

It is believed that even today, when Brahma says 'da,' it thunders, and he is trying to remind us of the three principles.

## 16 The Story of Uttanka

Sage Gautama's student Uttanka was very devoted. Gautama loved him very much and did not allow him to leave the ashram after completing his studies. When Uttanka grew too old to serve Gautama, he asked for permission to leave. Gautama agreed. He made Uttanka young again and married his daughter to him.

Before leaving, Uttanka asked Gautama's wife, what gift she would like as *gurudakshina*. She asked for the earrings that belonged to King Saudasa's wife. Uttanka went to Saudasa, who was living the life of a cannibal in a forest due to a curse. His wife gave Uttanka the earrings hoping that the good deed would remove the curse. She told Uttanka that the person who wore the earrings would be free from hunger and thirst and would be protected from danger.

While returning, Uttanka rested under a tree. A snake stole the earrings and entered an anthill. Uttanka started digging the anthill with his stick, but the kingdom of the snakes was very deep underground. Indra helped him by putting more power into his stick to help him dig faster. Agni, the god of fire, appeared in the form of a horse surrounded by fire and filled the kingdom of snakes with smoke. The snakes came out and to save their lives returned the earrings to Uttanka, who took them to Gautama's wife.

## 17 Vishvamitra

Once, King Kaushik, who was also called Vishvamitra, was touring his kingdom with his army. He reached the ashram of Sage Vashishtha, who invited him for meals. Vishvamitra asked him, "Do you have enough food to feed my army?" Vashishtha said that he had a cow called Nandini, who gave him anything he wanted. He asked Nandini to prepare a big feast for Vishvamitra and his army. Surprised at its powers, Vishvamitra said, "What will you do with this cow in this forest? This cow will be more useful to a king. Give me this cow as a gift." When Vashishtha did not agree to his demand, Vishvamitra forcefully captured the cow.

Separated from the sage who was like a father to her, Nandini was so sad that she

ran away from the king's palace. She went back to Sage Vashishtha who advised her to build her own army. Soon, Nandini created an army and defeated Vishvamitra. Vishvamitra then went to a forest to perform a long *tapasya* to get Nandini. After ten years of *tapasya*, Shiva was very pleased and gave him many weapons. Vishvamitra took all the weapons to fight Vashishtha. But he could not defeat Vashishtha because he absorbed all his weapons using one powerful weapon. Vishvamitra went back to the forest to perform more *tapasya*. He meditated for many years and became a *brahmarishi*. Now he had all the powers to get Nandini, but he had attained such mental peace that he no longer wanted the cow.

## 18 Satyavan and Savitri

Savitri, a princess, fell in love with a poor man called Satyavan. Narada Muni warned her not to marry Satyavan as he would die at an early age. He even told her when Satyavan was going to die. But Savitri was unmoved and married Satyavan.

On the day of Satyavan's death, she saw that Yama himself had come to take him. She begged Yama not to take Satyavan. But Yama said that no one could stop death.

Savitri followed them for miles and miles. Impressed with her determination, Yama said, "I will give you two boons; you can ask for anything except the life of Satyavan."

For the first boon, Savitri asked for the well-being of her father-in-law. For the second she cleverly asked for a hundred sons. Without thinking, Yama granted her the two boons. At this Savitri asked Yama to return her husband because without him, she could not have any sons. Defeated, Yama returned Savitri her husband.

## 19 Narasimha Avatar

Hiranyakashyap was a wicked king who prayed to Brahma for immortality. He requested that neither at day nor at night could any man, beast, god, or demon kill him. He also prayed that no instrument or weapon could ever destroy him. Impressed by his devotion, Brahma granted him the boon.

The king banned the worship of gods. But his son Prahlad was a devotee of Vishnu.

This enraged Hiranyakashyap and he decided to kill Prahlad. After many unsuccessful attempts, one evening, he ordered his men to tie Prahlad to a pillar and behead him. However, Vishnu took the form of Narasimha, a creature that was semi-man and semi-lion. He came out of the pillar and extended his sharp nails and tore Hiranyakashyap's chest apart and slashed his head.

## 20 The Intelligent Beggar

Two sages lived in an ashram. One day, after their prayers, when they were about to eat their food, a beggar came to them. He begged for food but the sages refused saying they had no food for him.

The beggar asked, "O respected saints, may I ask you, whom do you worship?" They replied, "We worship Pawan, the wind god, who is also *prana* (the breath of life)." He then asked, "Whom did you offer this food to before eating it yourself?" They said, "We offered it to Pawan or *prana*."

At this, the beggar said, "I hope you know that *prana* is present in all living creatures." The sages replied, "Yes, we know that." The beggar then said, "By denying food to me, you are denying food to *prana* who is present in me and for whom you have prepared it." The sages listened carefully to what the beggar was saying.

The sages were very ashamed at their ignorance and offered to share their food with the beggar.

## 21 Bharata, the Ideal Brother

Bharata left for Dandaka forest with an entire army of elephants, horses, cavalry, and priests to find Rama. When he saw Rama, he ran to him and begged forgiveness for his mother's behaviour and informed Rama about Dasaratha's death. The news greatly saddened Rama, Laxmana, and Sita. Then, Bharata pleaded, "I have come on behalf of the people of Ayodhya. Please accept the throne which lies empty without you." Rama answered, "I am only fulfilling our parents' wish." Bharata realised that Rama would not return to Ayodhya and said that he would place Rama's sandals on the throne and rule on his behalf. Rama gave Bharata his sandals. Bharata went back to Ayodhya and placed Rama's sandals on the throne.

## 22 How Kali Was Created

Kali is the fierce form of Durga or Parvati.

While fighting the demons, Durga realised that she would have to change herself into a violent and destructive force in order to kill the demons Chandra and Mundra.

In a fit of rage, Durga poured out lightening from her third eye. From this stark light a dark female figure was formed, with blazing eyes and disheveled hair, her red tongue shining bright. She did not wear diamonds or gold, rather a garland of human skulls, and cobras as bracelets. Armed with a trident, a sword, and a human skull in three hands respectively, she gave her blessings with her fourth hand.

Once created, the blood-thirsty goddess went on killing the demons. She killed Chandra and Mundra and earned the name of 'Chamundra.' Then Shiva appeared and threw himself at her feet to stop the rampage. Seeing Shiva at her feet, she realised her mistake and stopped the slaughter.

## 23 The Story of Yayati

Shukracharya was the guru of the demons. One day, his daughter Devyani was taking a bath in a lake with Sarmishtha, the daughter of the demon king, Vrishaparva. They had left their clothes on the bank. Suddenly a strong wind started blowing. They quickly came out of the lake and put their clothes on. By mistake, Sarmishtha wore Devyani's clothes. They started fighting. Sarmishtha pushed Devyani into a well and left her there.

After some time King Yayati passed by the well. Seeing Devyani, he pulled her out. They decided to get married. When Devyani did not return Shukracharya came looking for her. She refused to go back because the princess had insulted her. Shukracharya went to Vrishaparva and threatened to leave the kingdom. Vrishaparva begged Devyani for her forgiveness. Devyani agreed but on one condition—that Sarmishtha become her maid.

Soon Yayati and Devyani got married and had three sons. One day, Sarmishtha told Yayati how she came to be Devyani's maid. Sympathising with her, Yayati secretly married her and she had two sons. When Devyani came to know of their secret marriage, she told Shukracharya, who cursed Yayati with old age. Devyani was very sad at this. Shukracharya told her that it was not possible to take back the curse but a son of Yayati could exchange his youth with him.

Yayati requested each of his sons to take away his old age. Only his youngest son Puru agreed and Yayati become young again. After many years, he realised his injustice towards his son. He returned his son's youth and made him the king.

## 24 Birth of Saraswati

At the beginning of creation there was chaos all over. Brahma did not know how to bring order. While thinking over the problem he heard a voice say that knowledge could help him achieve order. So from Brahma's mouth emerged the magnificent figure of Saraswati—the goddess of knowledge and wisdom. Dressed in white, she rode on a swan, with books in one hand and the *veena*, a musical instrument, in the other.

By way of sense, thought, understanding, and communication she helped Brahma see how to change chaos into creation. When she played the *veena*, he heard the soothing music amidst the roar of commotion. Chaos started taking shape; the sun, the moon, and the stars were born. The oceans filled and seasons changed. The joyous Brahma then named Saraswati, Vagdevi, the goddess of speech and sound. Thus Brahma became the creator of the world with Saraswati as his source of wisdom.

## 25 The Great Teacher

One day the princes of Hastinapur were playing together and their ball fell into a well. Then a ring, too, fell into the well. The princes peered into the well but didn't know how to get them out.

Acharya Drona, who was standing nearby saw all this and said, "It is a shame that princes like you are not able to do such a small thing." He picked up a blade of grass and shot it at the ball in the well. The blade got stuck to the ball.

Then he shot another blade, which stuck to the end of the first blade. In this way, he made a chain of grass blades, which reached the top of the well.

He then pulled out the ball with it. Then he shot an arrow at the ring in the well. The arrow sprung back, and brought the ring with it. The princes were very happy.

Bhishma felt that Acharya Drona was skilled enough to teach the princes archery and warfare and later made him the princes' teacher.

## 26 Vamana Avatar

In Vishnu's fifth incarnation, he transforms himself into a *vamana* or dwarf.

Bali, the grandson of Prahlad, was a famous demon. By leading an austere life he had acquired the power to rule the earth. Indra and the other gods feared that some day Bali would conquer everything and defeat them. So they asked Vishnu for help.

Vishnu decided to be born in the household of a poor Brahmin. One day he went to Bali and asked for alms. Seeing the young boy, Bali agreed to give anything the dwarf asked for. Vamana asked for the entire land that would come under three steps. Bali agreed. The dwarf then grew in size and covered the earth and heavens with two steps. Due to lack of space he placed his third feet on Bali himself. He crushed Bali and sent him to the netherworld.

# 27 Shurpnakha

Many years passed. Rama, Laxmana, and Sita travelled through forests, meeting holy sages, and fighting demons. They finally arrived at Panchavati. Here they built a hut and passed their days happily.

One day, Ravana's sister, Shurpnakaha, who was wandering in the forests, spotted the handsome Rama outside his cottage and fell in love with him at first sight. Shurpnakha was very ugly. To attract Rama, she transformed herself into a beautiful maiden and approached him. She told him that she had fallen in love with him and wanted to marry him. He refused saying that he was already married.

Shurpnakha then spotted Laxmana and her feelings were aroused again seeing the equally handsome brother. She asked Laxmana, who also rejected her offer.

Shurpnakha could not bear this insult and attacked Sita. This angered Laxmana and he took a sword and cut off Shurpnakha's nose and ears.

# 28 Brahmarishi Vashishtha

Vashishtha, was the most legendary of all the eminent sages of India. Having conquered all his anger he became matchless in sacrifice and the scriptures. He was the royal priest of the Surya dynasty to which Rama was born. When Ravana captured him for not teaching him the Vedas, the sage cursed him saying that someone from this dynasty would kill him. Vashishtha's cow was the divine Kamadhenu, which became the cause for Vashishtha and Vishwamitra's rivalry when the latter tried to take it away. Even Vishwamitra had to bow down before this great ascetic's authority. Vashishtha was born thrice and in all the births Arundhati became his wife. He later became a 'saptarishi,' one of the seven revered sages who transformed into the constellation of seven stars called Ursa Major.

## 29  The Obedient Student

Eklavya was a tribal boy who wanted to learn to be a good archer. Acharya Drona, the royal teacher refused to teach him. Eklavya made a clay statue of Drona. Every day he practiced in front of the statue and soon became a good archer.

One day, when Eklavya was practicing, a dog started barking. He shot many arrows in its mouth. But he did it in such a manner that not a drop of blood came out. Drona, who was nearby, saw this and was impressed. He was sure that only a great archer could do that. He started searching for the archer and found Eklavya practicing nearby.

Drona went up to him and asked him, "Who is your teacher?" Eklavya answered, "You are my teacher," and showed him the statue. Drona said, "Give me your right thumb as my fees." Eklavya knew that without his right thumb he could not shoot, but he cut off his right thumb and gave it to his teacher.

## 30  Padmavati

Once Sage Bhrigu went to heaven and found Vishnu sleeping. He got angry and kicked his chest. Vishnu woke up and welcomed him. He said, "I am sorry, did you hurt your foot?" Brighu was pleased that Vishnu did not lose his temper. He blessed him and left. But Vishnu's wife, Parvati, was angry to know that the chest in which she resided was dishonoured. She immediately left Vishnu and went to earth. Vishnu was sad and followed by being born as Venkatesha.

One day, King Aksharaja was performing a ritual to be blessed with children, as a part of which he ploughed the earth. Suddenly a lotus came out bearing a baby girl in its petals. The king named the girl Padmavati and brought her up as his own daughter. This was actually Parvati, and when she grew up she was married to Venkatesha.

# 31 Bharathari

Bharathari was the youngest son of King Gandharva Sen of Ujjain. Gandharva Sen had two wives. Bharathari was born from the first wife and the second wife gave birth to Vikramaditya.

After the death of his father, Bharathari became the king since he was the eldest son. Later, he put his stepbrother Vikramaditya on the throne and lost interest in the welfare of the kingdom. He devoted his time to music, books, and the arts. He was also a great poet and a scholar of Sanskrit. When Vikramaditya saw Bharathari losing interest in the welfare of the people and the country, he urged him not to neglect his duties. Bharathari was furious and banished his stepbrother from the kingdom.

One day Bharathari found out that his wife was in love with the stable keeper. He became disillusioned and from that day onwards the king gave up all the pleasures of life. He began leading a holy life and chanting the name of Shiva. He realised that he had been selfish in thinking only about himself, and not about others.

In due course, he became free of worldly desires and attained *Shiva tatta* or complete self-knowledge. He followed the truth established in the Vedas.

Bharathari is regarded as one of the most respected sages of ancient India. He has always been praised by many sages and ascetics of India in different languages for his discipline and purity.

# Contents

*The Story of the Month:   The Descent of Ganga*

The Story of the Month

# The Descent of Ganga

## The Descent of Ganga

Once upon a time, long long ago, demons and gods were at war. To defeat the gods, the demons made a plan. During the day, they hid in the ocean and at night they attacked the gods. Afraid of being defeated in this way, the gods went to Sage Agastya for help.

Agastya solved their problem by drinking the whole ocean. Now as the demons had no place to hide, the gods easily defeated them. The gods then asked Agastya to bring the ocean back. Agastya said that he could not do that because he had already digested the ocean.

The people of the earth now had no water, as the ocean was empty. The gods were worried and went to Vishnu and requested him to bring water on earth. Vishnu assured them that river Ganga would come from the heaven to the earth.

In the meantime, on earth, King Sagara, who had sixty thousand sons, was performing a *yajna* to conquer the whole world. According to custom, he had sent out a white horse with an army. Wherever the horse went, the ruler of that kingdom would either have to fight with Sagara or give him his crown. In this way, Sagara was conquering the whole earth and wanted to be the most powerful. Indra, who was the ruler of heaven, was afraid that after conquering earth, Sagara would try to conquer heaven too.

To stop Sagara, Indra took the horse and hid it in Sage Kapila's ashram. Sagara sent his sons to search the horse. They reached Kapila's ashram. Sage Kapila was meditating and was disturbed. Greatly annoyed, with one look of his eyes, Kapila burnt all of them to ashes.

Sagara was very sad at the death of his sons. He wanted to purify the souls of his sons but only river Ganga could do that by washing their ashes. Ganga had to be brought

to earth. So Sagara performed *tapasya* to please Brahma. But he died before finishing the *tapasya*. His grandson then continued to perform the *tapasya*. This way, generation after generation performed the *tapasya*.

The seventh descendent of Sagara, Bhagiratha, was able to please Brahma. Brahma granted him his wish and asked Ganga to flow to earth. But Ganga didn't want to leave heaven and go to earth. She threatened to destroy all life on earth by the pressure of her flow. Only Shiva's powerful hair could control the force of

Ganga. Bhagiratha requested Shiva to help him. Shiva spread his hair and covered the sky. As soon as Ganga flowed down, he collected her water in his hair and tied it. Ganga flowed from his hair in the form of many small streams. She then followed Bhagiratha to the place where the ashes of his ancestors were lying. Being young Ganga flowed carelessly. She flooded the ashram of Sage Jahnu. Jahnu was performing a *yajna* at that time and the water put out all the fires. Angry Jahnu

swallowed Ganga. But when he came to know about the long *tapasya* that had been performed to bring Ganga to earth, he agreed to let her go. He cut open his left thigh and Ganga flowed out of it. Ganga came to be known as Jahnvi, the daughter of Jahnu.

Ganga flowed on and purified the ashes of Bhagiratha's ancestors. Therefore, Ganga is also called Bhagirathi. Thereafter, Ganga flowed and filled the empty ocean.

The ocean came to be known as Sagara after the name of King Sagara. The people of earth now had water to drink.

# 1 The Rich Man's Servant

As Vikram carried Betal on his shoulders, Betal started telling him a story.

There was once a very rich man called Dhaniram who was a miser and never donated money for charity. When his servant Rameshwar asked him to do some charity, Dhaniram said that he did not want to be known as a charitable person. So Rameshwar told Dhaniram, "Give me the money. I will use it for charity but will not tell anyone that you have donated it."

Dhaniram agreed and gave him some money. Rameshwar used it to set up a water tank for travellers. Everyone praised Rameshwar. He took more money from Dhaniram and built a small inn where travellers could rest. He again asked for money and this time made free food available at the inn.

One day, Dhaniram died and Rameshwar had no source of money. He started charging a fee for the services at the inn. The travellers who were used to the free services got very angry and killed Rameshwar.

Betal asked Vikram, "Tell me, who was responsible for the death of Rameshwar, Dhaniram or the travellers?" Vikram replied, "Rameshwar himself was responsible for his death. He should have made arrangements for the time when there would be no money to run the inn. Either he should have charged a small fee from the beginning or should not have charged anything even later." Betal said, "You are very wise. This is the right answer. But you answered the question so I will not go with you." Saying this, Betal flew back to his tree.

# 2 Krishna, the Shepherd Boy

As children, Krishna and his brother Balarama helped their father look after his cattle. Often, he and Balarama took the cattle to graze in the pastures of Gokul. While the cattle grazed, young Krishna played melodious tunes on his flute or played games with his friends.

One day while he and his friends were playing in the fields, Krishna noticed a new cow in his herd. He got alarmed and called Balarama. Krishna told him that the cow looked different and did not belong to them. Balarama agreed with Krishna.

Quietly, the brothers approached the cow. Krishna held the cow by his tail and whirled him around and threw him in the lake nearby.

Just as the cow fell, it transformed into a monster and died. Krishna told his friends that the monster had taken the form of a cow to kill him.

His friends rejoiced at the death of the monster and congratulated Krishna for his courage and strength.

## 3 Rama Kills Khara

Bruised, Shurpnakha rushed to her brothers Khara and Dushana. She narrated the incident and asked them to take revenge. Khara and Dushana were demon kings. Seeing Shurpnakha's plight, they became very angry. Meanwhile, Rama sensing some trouble, asked Laxmana to escort Sita to a secure place. He got ready with his bow and arrow. Khara and Dushana arrived with a strong army of elephants, horse-drawn chariots, and soldiers. The battle began. The enemies charged from all directions and Rama hit back with his powerful arrows. He destroyed the entire army. Finally, with one final shot he knocked down Khara, Dushana, and their friend Trisara. Meanwhile, one demon called Akampana, who survived the attack, rushed to Lanka to inform Ravana.

## 4 Drona's Test

Acharya Drona was the teacher of the princes of Hastinapur. Arjuna was his favourite student, so all the other students were jealous of him. To prove that Arjuna was the best student, Drona decided to conduct a test.

He hung a wooden bird from a tree and asked each prince to shoot at the bird's eye. First the eldest prince, Yudhishthira, was asked to try. When he aimed at the bird, Drona asked him, "What do you see in front of you?" Yudhishthira answered, "I see a tree and a bird hanging on it." Hearing this, Drona stopped him. He then asked other students the same question and got the same answer.

When it was Arjuna's turn and Drona asked him the same question, Arjuna replied, "I see only the bird's eye." Drona was very pleased with the answer and asked him to shoot. The arrow hit the bird's eye. Drona told all his students that the best archer is the one who can only see his target and nothing else.

## 5 Sage Agastya and the Demons

Ilvala and Vatapi were two demon brothers who hated all Brahmins. They thought of a devious plan by which they killed many Brahmins. The first one could take any form, and the second knew the secret of bringing the dead to life.

One day, they decided to kill the great sage, Agastya. They planned that Ilvala would turn into a goat and Vatapi would kill it and offer it to Agastya. Then using his powers he would bring him back to life. Ilvala would tear Agastya's stomach to come out, killing Agastya. Sage Agastya came to know of the wicked plan and decided to teach the two brothers a lesson. When Vatapi invited him to eat the meat, he decided to teach them a lesson. Agastya ate the goat meat, but before the demon could bring his brother back to life, he digested the meat, killing Ilvala.

## 6 Valmiki

Once there was a robber who looted travellers. One day, he tried to loot a traveller who had nothing. The traveller said, "I am Narada. Why do you commit the sin of robbing people?" The robber replied, "I have to support my family." Narada said, "Go and ask your family if they would share your sin like they share your loot." The robber went and asked his father, "I bring money by robbing people, will you share my guilt?" His father was furious and shouted, "Get lost, you robber!" His mother too was enraged and said, "Why should I? I never stole a thing in my life." His wife said, "It is your duty to support me." When he returned to Narada, the sage said, "Everybody is alone in this world. Worship God, it is he who stands by you always." The robber prayed for many years. Then he heard a voice from heaven, "Your new name is Valmiki and you will write the story of Rama." Valmiki wrote the *Ramayana*.

# 7 The Boys Who Never Grew Old

Sage Mrikandu prayed to Shiva for a son. Shiva appeared before him and asked, "Do you want an ordinary son or a perfect son who would not live more than sixteen years?"

Mrikandu thought, "If I ask for a perfect son, he would die at sixteen, but if I ask for an ordinary son, he would not be great." He chose a perfect son.

Soon his wife gave birth to a son whom they called Markandeya. He was a handsome, wise, and kind boy, perfect in every way.

A few days before his sixteenth birthday, Markandeya's parents told him that he would soon die. Markandeya said, "I will not die. I will pray to Shiva." He worshipped Shiva every day. On his sixteenth birthday, Yama, the god of death, came to take him. Markandeya said, "Let me

finish my prayer." Yama got angry and threw the noose over him. Shiva appeared and ordered him back to his kingdom saying, "Don't return to earth."

Yama went away. Nobody died on earth after that. The earth became overcrowded. Goddess Earth went to Shiva and said, "I am not able to carry this huge burden. Please send Yama to earth." When Lord Shiva refused, she went to Parvati for help. When Parvati repeated the request, Shiva said, "Yama has insulted my devotee." Parvati said, "But it was you who said that Markandeya would not be older than sixteen so Yama went to him." Shiva was in a fix. At this Parvati said, "Maybe you meant that Markandeya will always remain sixteen, but that foolish Yama misunderstood." Shiva was happy. He sent Yama to earth again. Markandeya always remained sixteen.

# 8 Padmanabha

Padmanabha, a devotee of Vishnu, belonged to a Brahmin family of Chakrapushkarini. Though poor, he was kind, honest, and just. He only wished to see the Almighty once. Yet he knew, that God did not appear before all. So Padmanabha absorbed himself in prayers. When his prayers reached their peak Vishnu appeared and blessed him with the boon of remaining alive through many ages. However, one day, a demon attacked

him. Fearing for his life he began taking the lord's name. Vishnu killed the demon with his *Sudarshan Chakra*, the divine wheel. This demon was the demi-god Sundar, whom Vasistha had cursed to change into a demon. He was to be freed only when Vishnu's *chakra* severed his head. Saluting the *chakra* for saving him Padmanabha prayed that it would protect mankind. The *chakra* entered the village of Pushkarini, which hence came to be known as Chakra-pushkarini.

# 9 The Royal Competition

One day, Drona decided to hold a competition in which the Kauravas and the Pandavas could display their skills. The princes demonstrated their expertise in using weapons like bow and arrow, sword, spear, and mace. There was a fierce mace fight between Bhima and Duryodhana. Arjuna impressed everyone by shooting blind-folded, creating fire and rain with arrows. Pleased, Drona declared that no one could match Arjuna. At this, a young man named Karna came forward and repeated everything that Arjuna had done. He challenged Arjuna. Drona said that an ordinary man could not compete with a prince. Duryodhana who was jealous of Arjuna immediately declared Karna the king of Angadesha. But the fight could not take place as the sun had set. Karna was actually a son of Kunti, the mother of the Pandavas.

# 10 Akampan Goes to Ravana

Akampan, who was at the battlefield at the time of Khara's death, rushed to inform Ravana.

Ravana seethed with anger while Akampan narrated the incident. He demanded to know the name of the person who dared to kill his brothers and injure his sister, Shurpnakha.

Frightened, Akampan told him about Rama and the powers he possessed.

Ravana wanted to kill Rama immediately but Akampan warned him. He said that Rama was very powerful and so they had to think of a plan to kill him.

He informed Ravana about Rama's beautiful wife Sita. He said that both Rama and Sita loved each other deeply and if Sita was harmed in any way, Rama would surely come to save her.

Ravana liked Akampan's idea very much and decided to abduct Sita.

# 11 Mahakaleshwar

Once there was a Brahmin who worshipped Shiva. Dushan, a demon, had become powerful because of a boon granted by Brahma. He started disturbing the Brahmin during his meditation. Shiva appeared and burnt Dushan. After this, Shiva was given the name *Mahakaal* and a *Jyotirlinga* (shrine where Shiva is worshipped) called Mahakaaleshwar was set up in Ujjain.

## 12 Ganesha and Kubera

Kubera, the god of wealth, once visited Shiva and Parvati in Mount Kailash. He wanted to show off his wealth, so he invited them to a meal. Shiva and Parvati said, "We cannot come, but you may take Ganesha. But he eats a lot." Kubera said, "He can eat as much as he wants." When the child sat down to eat, he ate all the food. But he remained hungry, so he ate the utensils, the furniture, and the palace. Still he went on eating and ate Kubera's entire kingdom. Kubera begged him to stop but he threatened, "If you don't give me food, I will eat you." Kubera went to Shiva for help. He apologised for his pride. Shiva gave him a handful of rice to give to Ganesha. Kubera went back and offered the rice to Ganesha with love and humility. Ganesha's hunger was satisfied.

## 13 Narada Muni

Narada Muni was a *gandharva,* a nature spirit that is part animal. During a sacrifice, seeing the beautiful maidens, his mind wandered. This wrongful act angered Parvati's father, Dakshabrahma, who cursed him to be born to a maidservant.

In his next birth, Narada and his mother began serving the sages. Pleased with their service, the gods allowed them to taste their food. The saintly food purified their hearts and Narada became their student.

After his mother's death, he headed for the forests in search of the lord. One day, he saw a vision of the Almighty, which said, "As you have seen me once your desire to be with me shall grow. You shall join me in heaven one day."

After his death, he took the form of a heavenly being and joined the lord.

# 14 Saturn

A Brahmin named Haridas, once heard a voice that said, "I will trouble your king for seven and a half hours." Haridas was frightened and told his wife what he had heard. She knew that it was the voice of Saturn, so she said, "You must protect the king and take the trouble on yourself." When Haridas heard the voice again, he offered to take the trouble on himself. Saturn agreed and said, "Your period of trouble starts now."

One day, Haridas went to the river to pray. He found two watermelons, which he took home. Meanwhile, the two princes were found to be missing. When the soldiers came looking for them, Saturn made Haridas's watermelons look like the heads of the princes. They arrested Haridas for murdering the princes. The king ordered Haridas to be hanged. But just before he could be hanged, his period of trouble was over. The princes returned safely and Haridas was saved.

# 15 Laxmi, Saraswati, and Vishnu

While Brahma created the universe, the planets, the stars, and life on earth, he gave it order and harmony. Now it was upon Vishnu to maintain this balance and order. Vishnu approached Saraswati to use her knowledge to maintain the order of creation and harmony between animals and man. But he realised that to maintain harmony, there has to be growth and prosperity and only Laxmi, could provide that. So Vishnu asked for Laxmi's help. Now the question arose who was greater, Laxmi or Saraswati, wealth or knowledge. Laxmi and Sarswati argued between themselves as to who was greater. Seeing their argument, Vishnu intervened. He explained that with knowledge he can read and write, but without wealth he cannot buy the tools like books and pen to gain that knowledge.

# 16 Ashtavakra

Kahoda studied the holy verses. His unborn son learnt many verses in his mother's womb. Once when Kahoda was teaching his class, the baby spoke, "Father, you are saying the verse wrong." Kahoda cursed him that he would be born deformed. Once King Janak wanted to perform a *yajna*, but Sage Bandhi stopped it. He declared that someone had to defeat him in the debate of holy verses. Whoever was defeated would be drowned in the river.

Kahoda tried but was defeated. Kahoda's son was born with eight bends in his body and was named 'Ashtavakra.' He defeated Bandhi in the debate. Bandhi then revealed that he was Varuna, the god of water's son. Varuna was performing a *yajna* in heaven for which he needed sages. By drowning the sages Bandhi had sent them to heaven. As the *yajna* was complete all the sages came out of the river. Bandhi asked Ashtavakra to take a dip in the river and when he came out his body had straightened.

# 17 The King's Judgement

Once again, Vikram got Betal down from the tree. As he was carrying him, Betal narrated another story. King Chandradeva was a just king. One day, a neighbouring king threatened to attack him. Chandradeva did not want a war because it would lead to the death of many of his soldiers. Chandradeva asked the neighbouring king to fight with him. Whoever won, could take over the other's kingdom. The neighbouring king agreed. Chandradeva won but he did not take over the neighbouring kingdom and spared the king's life.

After a few days, Chandradeva went to a forest, where a lion attacked him. A thief who was hiding in the forest saved his life. The thief hoped that Chandradeva would reward him. Instead Chandradeva had him hanged.

Betal asked Vikram, "Chandradeva spared the neighbouring king who was his enemy and hanged the thief who saved his life. Was the king's judgement right?"

Vikram replied, "Chandradeva was right in his judgement. A king's first duty is to think about the welfare of his kingdom. By forgiving the neighbouring king, he prevented future war and ensured peace for his kingdom. By hanging the thief he made sure that there would be no thefts in his kingdom."

Betal said, "You are right. But you broke your silence and here I go." Betal flew back to his tree.

# 18 Lord Vishnu's Love for His Devotee

King Ambrish observed a three-day fast to worship Vishnu. Before breaking it, he invited sages and Brahmins for a feast.

Sage Durvasa also came. Durvasa said, "I will eat only after taking a bath in the river." All the guests waited for Durvasa. But he took a long time and it was almost noon. The Brahmins told Ambrish that if he didn't break his fast before noon, it would be a sin. Ambrish said, "If I eat before Durvasa, he will feel insulted." The Brahmins suggested, "Have water to break the fast now and you can have food when Durvasa returns. This would save you from both—sinning, and insulting Durvasa."

Just as Ambrish was about to drink water, Durvasa returned. In anger he shouted,

"How dare you break your fast without me?" Durvasa threw a *chakra* towards Ambrish, who ran to save his life. Ambrish went to Vishnu for help. Vishnu sent out his *chakra*. It destroyed Durvasa's *chakra* and started chasing him. Durvasa was terrified and ran over hills and valleys, but the *chakra* continued to follow him. He went to Brahma, who could not help him. He then went to

Shiva, who asked him to go to Vishnu. But Vishnu said, "You have insulted my devotee. Only he can forgive you." Finally Durvasa went to Ambrish and begged for his life. Ambrish prayed to Vishnu and the *chakra* immediately disappeared.

Ambrish told Durvasa that it was Vishnu's love for his devotee that had given him the power to do that.

# 19 The Story of Tuesday

Mangal, the god with the red body, is worshipped on a Tuesday. He tests his devotees time and again, and a rigorous fast on a Tuesday relieves one of all obstacles in life.

One day, an old lady was performing her fast. A devout worshipper, she had named her son Mangaliya. Wanting to test her faith, Mangal appeared in the guise of a poor Brahmin. He wanted the old lady to cook some rice for him. The lady refused saying that she could

not cook on a Tuesday. The Brahmin then asked her to prepare the cow-dung plastered pit for the fire to be lit. The lady refused to touch the cow dung on a Tuesday.

The angry Brahmin then said that he would light the fire on her son's back. She begged for her son's life. However knowing that breaking a fast brings great misfortune she called her son.

Seeing her devotion, Mangal changed back into his true form and blessed her and went away.

## 20 Krishna Kills Aghasura

The gods were anxiously waiting for someone powerful to kill the deadly demon, Aghasura. Aghasura on the other hand wanted to avenge the killing of his siblings, Putana and Bakasura, by Krishna. So he decided to use his great mystic powers. Changing himself into a gigantic black serpent he arrived before Krishna and his friends. Seeing the enormous creature which had fiery eyes and was breathing hotly , the boys grew curious. Its mouth expanded from the skies to the land. Wanting to probe further, the boys entered its mouth. But Aghasura was waiting for Krishna. Finally, Krishna stepped in and Aghasura snapped his jaws so hard that it nearly crushed the boys. Krishna instantly expanded his body so that it choked the serpent, which died in seconds.

## 21 Maharishi Bhrigu and Vishnu

Once a debate arose as to who among Brahma, Shiva, and Vishnu was the greatest. After much thought, it was decided that the noble sage, Bhrigu, would be sent to test the three gods.

Bhrigu first went to Brahma, but did not pay his respects to him. Brahma felt very insulted at this behaviour.

His next destination was Mount Kailash, where Shiva resided. He told Shiva that he was not happy with his ways.

The god, who was known for his violent temper, chased Bhrigu with a trident. Somehow managing to escape, Bhrigu reached Vaikunthloka where Vishnu was reclining on Seshnag.

Bhrigu kicked Vishnu on his chest. Startled, Vishnu awoke and begged forgiveness and said, "Kindly allow me to nurse your feet which hit against my hard chest."

Seeing Vishnu's concern and care, Bhrigu and the sages declared him the greatest of the gods.

## 22 The Forest Fire

After slaying Kaliya, Krishna and his people were on their way back through a forest. As night fell it became impossible to return home. So they decided to spend the night in the forest.

After a while a great forest fire started. Spreading wildly it began scorching the entire forest.

Scared, the people ran to Krishna to save them from the raging fire. They knew that only Krishna, who possessed great powers, could save them.

Krishna looked at the fire blazing in the distance. He stood firm and as it came close, opened his mouth wide, and swallowed the destructive forest fire.

Amazed by his strength, the people rejoiced and hailed the lord with praise.

## 23 Lord Vishnu and Markandeya

Markandeya was a great devotee of Lord Vishnu. One day, he left his home to live on a mountain by the Pushpabhadra River. He prayed to Vishnu day and night. Vishnu was pleased with his devotion and decided to reward Markandeya.

One day, Markandeya saw thick black clouds forming. Soon, it started raining heavily, covering the entire mountain. There was chaos all around and Markandeya felt lost. He was very scared and climbed a tree. To his astonishment, he found a baby lying on a branch of the tree. The baby sucked him into his mouth. Markandeya saw the entire universe: the sky, the earth, the heavens, the seas, and the mountains. He saw forests, rivers, cities, and people. He was amazed. Just then the baby exhaled and Markandeya came back to the tree.

Markandeya realised that he had just seen the greatness of Vishnu.

# 24 Trishanku's Heaven

King Trishanku went to his guru Vashishtha and said, "Please help me perform a ritual by which I can go to heaven while I am still alive." Vashishtha replied, " It is a law that no living person can go to heaven. Go and do good deeds and you will go to heaven when you die." Disappointed, Trishanku requested Vashishtha's sons to help him. They got angry, "How can you ask us something that our father has already denied? We curse you to become old." Trishanku immediately turned old. He went to the great sage, Vishwamitra, for help. Vishwamitra promised to fulfil his wish. Vishwamitra performed a big *yajna*; he chanted mantras and made offerings to gods. But the gods did not want anyone to break a law and enter heaven alive; they did not accept the offerings.

Vishwamitra was furious and said, "I will send you to heaven by my own powers. Rise Trishanku." As he said this, Trishanku began to rise and reached the gates of heaven. The gods stopped him and said, "You can't come to heaven alive. Fall back to earth."

Trishanku started falling back. Vishwamitra said, "Don't fall! Stay!" And Trishanku hung between heaven and earth. Then Vishwamitra said,

"I will create another heaven for Trishanku." He created the stars and as he was going to create another Indra, the gods stopped him saying, "Don't do this unnatural thing." By this time, Vishwamitra had cooled down. He agreed to stop but said, "I have to keep my promise. Trishanku will live with these stars." The gods agreed but declared that Trishanku would live in his heaven upside down.

# 25 The Trembling of the Earth

The gods, demons, kings, and sages had assembled at Mount Kailash for the wedding of Shiva and Parvati.

Suddenly, the earth began to tremble and shake vigorously. Everyone got alarmed and thought that the end was near. Shiva said, "All of you have assembled on Kailash, which is in the north. Because all the weight is at one place, the earth has become heavy on one side. To solve this problem, somebody needs to go to

the south and balance the earth with his weight. Only Agastya's *tapasya* has such weight." He asked Agastya to save the world. Agastya wanted to attend the wedding like the others. Shiva understood his dilemma and said, "Do your duty and whenever you think of me and Parvati, we will appear before you."

Agastya was happy; he went to the south and sat on the top of a mountain to perform his *tapasya*. The earth was stable again and the wedding went on smoothly.

## 26 Balarama and Dhenukasura

Krishna's brother, Balarama, was also very powerful.

One day, his friends came crying for help. They told him that they wanted to enter the beautiful forest of Talavana, which was captured by the ass-demon Dhenukasura and his friends.

Balarama assured his friends that they would be able to enter Talvana and eat its ripe fruits. He entered the forest and in a great show of strength began felling the trees with his arms. Hearing the noise, Dhenukasura emerged and came charging at Balarama.

He kicked him violently with his hind legs, but Balarama did not move. After some time, he caught the ass by its hind legs, swung it around and threw it on the treetop killing Dhenukasura. To take revenge, Dhenukasura's friends gathered. Balarama and Krishna tossed them too and the forest was safe again.

## 27 Shurpnakha Goes to Ravana

When Shurpnakha heard the news that Ravana had dropped the idea of taking revenge, she rushed to him. The sight of Shurpnakha with a bleeding nose and severed ears aroused Ravana's pity. Weeping bitterly, Shurpnakha told Ravana that Rama attacked her because she had wanted to gift Sita to Ravana to make his queen. Knowing Ravana's liking for beautiful women, she also described Sita's beauty, thereby arousing his curiosity about her. Shurpnakha's words hurt Ravana's pride. To increase his anger, she said it did not suit Ravana to sit with folded arms, scared of an ordinary man like Rama. She urged him to take revenge for this dreadful act. Before taking leave, Shurpnakha also gave hints about abducting Sita from Panchavati, but warned him about Laxmana, Rama's devoted brother, who always guarded Sita.

## 28 Saraswati Saves the World

Once Shiva saw the world filled with evil. He decided to clean it and opened his third eye from which came a great fire. Saraswati took the form of a river and absorbed the fire. She took it into the sea where it formed a fire-spitting creature called Badavagni. Saraswati declared, "As long as man is wise, this animal will remain here, but if man becomes corrupt, this beast will destroy the world."

## 29 Suteekshna's Gurudakshina

Suteekshana was a student of Sage Agastya. When he completed his education, he asked Agastya what *gurudakshina* (fees) he should give.

Agastya asked Suteekshana to help him see God. Suteekshana made an ashram for himself in the Dandaka forest. He had heard that Rama, the incarnation of Vishnu, would pass through Dandaka forest during his exile. So he waited there singing in praise of God.

One day, he heard that Rama had arrived in Dandaka. Suteekshana was so absorbed in the vision of Vishnu that when Rama called him he did not hear him at first. After his meditation was over, when he opened his eyes, he found Rama, Sita, and Laxmana standing before him. He was overjoyed to see them. He took them to his teacher Agastya's ashram and fulfilled his promise.

## 30 Krishna and Sankhasura

Sankhasura, the demon with a conch-shaped jewel on his head, was very proud. He felt that because of his riches women would love him. He was jealous of Krishna because he thought he was an ordinary cowherd who always enjoyed the company of the *gopis*. One night, Krishna and Balarama accompanied by the pretty maidens, were performing the *raasleela,* a type of dance. See-ing this, Sankhasura was jealous. He started pulling out the young girls from the performance. The maidens screamed for help. Krishna stopped Sanskha-sura. He rescued the girls and asked Balarama to look after them. Seeing Krishna's might, Sankhasura ran for his life. However, Krishna grabbed him and knocked him down with a strong blow. As Sankhasura writhed in pain, Krishna took out the conch-shaped jewel and offered it to Balarama.

# Contents

*The Story of the Month:  Sita's Abduction*

The Story of the Month

# Sita's Abduction

# Sita's Abduction

Ravana, the king of demons, was the ruler of Lanka. He had heard many stories about Rama's wife, Sita's beauty. He decided to kidnap Sita and bring her to Lanka. He made a plan to abduct her and went to his uncle, Mareecha, a demon, and asked for his help. Mareecha had the power to transform himself into any form and even change his voice accordingly. He had heard about the greatness of Rama and tried to discourage Ravana. He advised him to stay away from Rama as that would only lead to the downfall of Lanka but Ravana was furious and determined. He threatened to kill

Mareecha. Mareecha was left with no choice and reluctantly agreed to help Ravana. According to Ravana's plan, Mareecha transformed himself into a golden deer and went to graze near the hermitage where Rama and Sita, along with Laxmana, were staying.

When Sita saw the beautiful deer, she was fascinated by its beauty and asked Rama to bring it for her. Rama and Laxmana had never seen a deer like this before and Laxmana warned Rama that the deer might be a demon in disguise. But Sita had set her heart on the golden deer and was adamant.

At her insistence, Rama went after the deer. He asked Laxmana to stay with Sita and protect her while he went after the deer. The deer ran deeper and deeper into the forest and Rama followed it. Finally, Rama aimed an arrow at the deer's heart and shot it. When the arrow struck the deer, it transformed itself back into Mareecha. He cried out to Laxmana for help in Rama's voice and then died. When Sita and Laxmana heard Rama's voice crying for help, they got alarmed. Sita begged Laxmana to go and see if Rama was in trouble.

Laxmana was in a dilemma. On the one hand, he had promised Rama that he would stay with Sita and protect her, and on the other hand, he was worried about his brother and wanted to go and see if Rama needed his help. He tried to put Sita's fears at rest but she was inconsolable and forced Laxmana to go in search of Rama. Laxmana agreed to go but wanted to make sure that Sita would be safe during his absence. He drew a line around the hut with his arrow and told Sita not to step out of the line. He said that if she stayed within the boundary of the line, no harm would come to her.

Meanwhile, Ravana was hiding nearby and had heard Laxmana and Sita talking. He saw Làxmana drawing a line around the hut and heard him instructing Sita not to step out. Soon after Laxmana left, Ravana quickly disguised himself as an old hermit and approached the hut. He begged for some alms and food. Sita was very kind hearted and brought food and water for the elderly hermit and offered it to him. Ravana wanted Sita to step out of the line drawn by Laxmana. He told her that he could hardly reach the water and requested her to step forward and give it to him. Sita thought that he was a harmless, weak hermit and did not want to annoy him so she stepped out of the circle.

As soon as she had done so, Ravana grabbed her and revealed his true identity. He told her that he was the king of Lanka and had come to take her with him to his land. Sita was terrified and told Ravana that Rama and Laxmana would find her and punish Ravana for abducting her. She struggled hard, but in vain. Ravana was very strong and quickly overpowered her. He laughed at her and mercilessly dragged her into his flying chariot and took her away to Lanka.

# 1 Ajamil Turns a New Leaf

Ajamil was the son of a devout devotee of Vishnu. But, unlike his holy father, Ajamil was lazy and wasted his time in sinful activities.

One day, his father sent him to the nearby forest to pluck flowers. There a beautiful tribal woman, accompanied by her lover, saw the handsome Ajamil and fell in love with him. She approached him and expressed her wish to be his wife. Ajamil who was equally charmed by her beauty also agreed to marry her and soon they were married.

Ajamil returned home with his bride. Shocked, his father rejected her saying that she had sinned. A heated argument followed between Ajamil and his father after which he threw the old man on the ground and asked him to leave the house. Many years passed and Ajamil's sins only increased day by day. He drank heavily and gambled in bad company.

Ajamil's wife bore him ten sons. The youngest, called Narayana was the most loved of them all.

Ajamil slowly became poor in health and took to his bed. Frail and ailing, he saw Yama's two messengers by his bedside. Startled, he shouted his son Narayana's name. Vishnu who is also called Narayana, heard the plea and responded.

He immediately sent his men to tell Yamraj to delay Ajamil's death. Yamraj agreed.

Meanwhile Ajamil thanked Vishnu for saving his life and drowned himself in prayers. He gave up all corrupt activities and became a pious man.

Seeing Ajamil change his bad ways, Vishnu blessed him.

# 2 Balarama and Pralambasura

One day, while engaged in a playful pastime, Krishna and Balarama saw the demon, Pralambasura, enter the fields in the hope of kidnapping them.

Krishna wondered how to kill the demon. Instead of attacking him, he welcomed Pralambasura into their game.

Krishna decided to form two teams, one led by him, the other by Balarama. He would then invite a member from each team to fight a duel. Afterwards the winners would be rewarded with a ride on the loser's back. Pralambasura took Krishna's side, but Krishna decided to purposefully lose the game. Meanwhile, Pralambasura, thinking Balarama to be weak, decided to carry him on his shoulders. He carried him far into the jungles and there changed into an enormous giant who nearly touched the skies. Balarama, seeing Pralambasura's changing form, also grew in size. Like a mountain, he rose up on the demon's back and struck his neck. Pralambasura died on the spot.

# 3 Jatayu

On their way to Panchavati, Rama, Laxmana, and Sita had seen a huge vulture swooping down towards them. Rama had confronted him and asked who he was. The bird had saluted them and said he was Jatayu, King Dasaratha's friend. He had protected him during the battle with Samparasura. Rama had welcomed his father's saviour.

Then Jatayu had narrated this story. He said that he was the grandson of Sage Kashyap and his father Arun was the charioteer of the sun god Surya. He had also told them how his elder brother Sampati had burnt his wings while trying to save him from soaring towards the sun. He had come to the forest of Panchavati where he was entrusted with the kingship of the vultures. Jatayu had promised Rama that he would protect them with all his might.

# 4 Vikram, Betal, and the Kind Sage

Once more Betal was narrating another story. A king took his son to a sage and said, "Take him as your student but make sure that he is treated like a prince." The sage said, "If I am to teach him, he will be treated as any other student." This made the king angry. He resolved to teach the sage a lesson. When the prince completed his education, he asked his teacher, "Sir, what *guru-daskshina* (fees) should I give you?" The sage replied, "I will ask for my fees when the time comes."

When the prince returned, the king asked his men to burn down the sage's ashram. The prince got very angry when he saw the burnt ashram. He said, "I will kill the person who has done this." Hearing this, the sage asked him for his fees. Betal asked Vikram, "What did he ask for?" Vikram said, "The sage asked the prince to forgive the king." Betal said, "You are right, but you opened your mouth, so here I go."

# 5 Mandodari

Maya, the king of giants, married Hema, the beautiful fairy, who bore him a daughter, Mandodari. Hema had no affection for her husband or Mandodari, and finally she abandoned them and left for the heavens.

Maya wandered in the forests with the baby in his arms. After nearly fifteen years, he suddenly realised that his baby had blossomed into a beautiful girl. Once, they met Ravana in a dense forest where he was captivated by Mandodari's beauty. Introducing himself to Maya, Ravana told him about his rich ancestors and asked for Mandodari's hand in marriage. Maya graciously accepted Ravana as his son-in-law. Though she became Ravana's most beloved wife, Mandodari never hesitated to warn him of his misdeeds.

# 6 The Lac Palace

Yudhisthira, the eldest Pandava, was made the *yuvraja*(crown prince) of Hastinapur as he was the eldest prince. This made Duryodhana jealous. With the help of his uncle, Shakuni, he made a plan to kill the Pandavas. They persuaded the Pandavas to attend a grand fair in the town of Varnavat. Duryodhana had a lac palace built for them. Lac burns very easily. He had planned that when the Pandavas were sleeping in the palace, one of his men would set it on fire and they would be burnt to death. Vidura, the prime minister, came to know of this plot and warned the Pandavas. He also had a secret tunnel dug, through which the Pandavas could escape. The Pandavas and their mother Kunti, stayed in the palace during their visit. But Bhima himself set the palace on fire. The Pandavas safely escaped through the tunnel and Duryodhana thought that they had died in the fire.

## 7 Bhima and Hidimba

After the lac palace incident, the Pandavas went to a forest. After walking for a long time, they came to the part of the forest where a demon named Hidimb and his sister Hidimba lived.

Kunti and four of the Pandavas were tired and fell asleep; Bhima was awake and kept a watch. Hidimb sensed the smell of human beings and asked Hidimba to go after them. As soon as Hidimba saw the handsome Bhima, she fell in love with him. She took the form of a beautiful woman and went to him. She said, "I am Hidimba, my brother is a demon, he will eat all of you." Bhima smiled and replied, "Don't worry, I am strong enough to defeat your brother."

When Hidimba did not return for a long time, Hidimb

went looking for her and saw her talking to Bhima. He was furious and shouted, "I sent you to kill the human and you are talking to him. I will kill him myself." Saying so, he attacked Bhima. A fierce fight followed and ended with Bhima killing Hidimb. The thunderous roars of the two fighters woke the four Pandavas and Kunti. Hidimba told them that she was a demoness and wished to marry Bhima.

With Kunti's permission the marriage took place. After some time Hidimba gave birth to a son who was named Ghatotkacha.

After a few years, Kunti and the Pandavas decided to leave that part of the forest. They took leave of Hidimba and Ghatotkacha, who had grown up to be a strong boy. He promised the Pandavas that he would come to them, whenever they needed him.

## 8 Manu and the Fish

One day, King Manu was collecting water from a river when a small fish swam into his vessel. As he tried to throw it back, the small fish begged him to save it from the big fish. The king took pity on the fish and kept it in a bowl of water. By the next morning, the fish had grown big so Manu kept it in a tank.

Day after day, the fish kept growing in size and finally it was so big that it had to be taken to the ocean. As Manu

was putting the fish in the ocean, the fish told him, "I am Matsya, the avatar of Vishnu. In a few days, a big flood will submerge the whole earth. You must build a big ship and fill it with good people and animals and plants of all kind."

As the fish had predicted, it rained continuously for seven days and seven nights and all the creatures drowned in the flood except those who were on Manu's ship. Manu created a new kingdom on earth with the creatures who had survived.

## 9 Jatayu Fights Ravana

When Ravana was taking Sita away to Lanka in his flying chariot, Jatayu, the wise old bird, was resting in the forest. Hearing Sita's helpless screams, Jatayu flew to Ravana's chariot.

Jatayu was a great devotee of Rama. He could not keep quiet at the plight of Sita, although the wise bird knew that he was no match for the mighty Ravana. But he was not afraid of Ravana's strength even though he knew that he would get killed by obstructing the path of Ravana. Jatayu decided to save Sita from the clutches of Ravana at any cost. He stopped Ravana and ordered him to leave Sita, but Ravana threatened to kill him if he interfered. Chanting Rama's name, Jatayu attacked Ravana with his sharp claws and hooked beak.

His sharp nails and the beak tore flesh from the body of Ravana. Ravana took out his diamond-studded arrow and fired at Jatayu's wings. As the arrow hit, the frail wing tore off and fell, but the brave bird continued fighting. With his other wing he bruised Ravana's face and tried to pull Sita from the chariot. The fight went on for quite some time. Soon, Jatayu was bleeding from the wounds all over his body.

Finally, Ravana took out one huge arrow and shot Jatayu's other wing as well. As it hit, the bird fell on the ground, bruised and battered.

Jatayu wanted to meet Rama in his last moments before he died and tell him about Sita. So, even while he was dying, he went on repeating the name of Rama.

## 10 King Satyapal's Wisdom

Betal narrated the story of King Satyapal to Vikram. When Satyapal ascended the throne of Chandadesh, the Bhil tribes were fighting for independence from Chandadesh. The country was poor and was under threat from Prachand Verma, a neighbouring king.

Satyapal went to his ministers, who suggested that he should marry Prachand's daughter. Satyapal refused because Prachand's daughter considered him a weak king.

One day, he met Kirtisena, the princess of the Bhils. Following her advice, Satyapal ousted his corrupt ministers and became prosperous again. Then, he met the Bhil king and asked for Kirtisena's hand in marriage. Having gained the faith of the Bhils, he now attacked Prachand and vanquished him.

Betal asked Vikram "Was Satyapal's strategy right?" Vikram replied "It was perfect because Satyapal put his house in order first before facing his enemies."

# 11 Jatayu Helps Rama

As Rama discovered the deceit of Mareecha, he grew anxious about Sita and Laxmana. Running through the dense forest, he called out their names. After some time, he saw Laxmana, and told him about Mareecha's deceit—how, by imitating Rama's voice, he had got Laxmana to come out, leaving Sita behind. Anxious that something terrible might have happened to Sita, the brothers rushed home. On reaching, they found the door ajar and the fruits scattered. Sita was nowhere in sight. They began a frantic search through the forests. Suddenly, they chanced upon the injured Jatayu. Writhing in pain, the bird just managed to tell them about Sita's abduction and pointed to the direction in which Ravana had gone. With folded wings, he bid goodbye and breathed his last.

# 12 Krishna Saves Nanda

One day Nanda went to take a dip in the Yamuna at an unfavorable time.

Seeing Nanda in the river at such an odd hour, the attendants of Varuna, the sea god, arrested him and took him to their master.

Nanda's friends went to Krishna for help, who immediately left for Varuna's abode. Elated to see Krishna, Varuna immediately released Nanda and begged him to forgive his servants.

## 13 Narada and Ved Vyasa

Long long ago, Sage Ved Vyasa had written the Puranas to explain the meaning of Vedas to the common people.

One day, he sat thinking what to write next. Just then, Sage Narada came to him with a suggestion. He said, "You should write about the glory of Narayana to inspire *bhakti* (devotion) in people. It is because of *bhakti* towards Narayana that I am his attendant. In my previous birth I was an angel in heaven. Once,

Dakshabrahma was performing a *yajna*. Since I was not paying attention to the mantras, he cursed me to be born as a human. So I was born as the son of a servant in an ashram. In the company of the sages of the ashram, I developed devotion to god. I went to meditate in the forest. After many years, Narayana appeared before me and promised to make me his attendant in my next life."

Inspired by Sage Narada's story, Ved Vyasa wrote the *Mahabharata*.

## 14 Birth of Draupadi

King Drupada and Acharya Drona were enemies. One day, Drupada asked two sages, Yaja and Upayaja, to perform a *yajna* that could give Drupada a son who could kill Drona. When the *yajna* was over, the sages offered the

prasada to Drupada's wife. At that moment, the queen had something in her mouth so she asked the sages to wait. They got angry and Yaja put the *prasada* in the *yajna* fire. Suddenly from the fire emerged a young warrior. In anger, Upayaja also put the *prasada* in the fire. Suddenly,

a beautiful woman came out of the fire. A voice was heard from the sky, "This woman has taken birth to become the cause of destruction of those who are evil." The woman came to be known as Draupadi after her father Drupada and the warrior was called Dhrishtadhyumna.

## 15 Nahusha's Pride

King Nahusha performed hundred *ashwamedha yajnas* and conquered all the kingdoms of earth and heaven. He dethroned Indra to become the king of heaven. Then, Nahusha ordered Indra and his wife Shachi to become his servants.

Shachi, who was the queen of heaven, did not want to become a servant. She thought of a plan to punish Nahusha. She told Nahusha that she and Indra would become his servants only if he came on a palanquin carried by sages. She knew that sages are great people who would be insulted if Nahusha asked them to carry a palanquin. Proud Nahusha failed to realise this and ordered a few sages to carry his palanquin. Agastya was one of the sages carrying the palanquin. Agastya was short and because of this the palanquin tilted to one side. At this, Nahusha got angry and kicked him. Agastya felt insulted and cursed him to be born as a snake.

## 16 Durgam and the Vedas

Durgam, the king of the demons once asked his minister, "Why is it that the gods are always able to win over us? They must have secret powers."

He replied, "The gods have the knowledge of Vedas which gives them great powers."

Durgam decided to get the Vedas and performed a long *tapasya*. When Brahma appeared he requested him to make him the protector of the Vedas. But instead of protecting them, he took and hid them in *patal-lok* (netherworld).

The *yajnas* performed with the help of the Vedas used to help the gods and sages remain young and glowing but now that they were lost the gods and sages became old and weak. On earth, drought and famine occurred because no *yajnas* were performed to cause rain. There was death and destruction everywhere. Terrified, the gods went to Vishnu for help. He asked them to worship Jagatmata Ma Bhagwati. The gods begged her for help. Ma Bhagwati gave them a leaf that had grown on her body. With this leaf, it rained on earth and prosperity was restored. Then Ma Bhagwati formed ten goddesses—Kali, Tara, Chinnamstaka, Shrividya, Bhuvaneshwari, Bhairavi, Bagula, Dhrumra, Tripura, and Matangi from her body. With these goddesses she attacked Durgam and defeated him. The Vedas were restored to the gods and sages.

# 17 Tapti

One day, King Panchal attacked the kingdom of King Sarvan. Panchal's army was bigger and stronger and soon defeated Sarvan's army. Sarvan had to leave his kingdom; he started living in the forest. One day, Sage Vashishtha came to his home. Sarvan asked the sage to bless him so that he could win his kingdom back. Sarvan collected his army and challenged Panchal to a battle. He fought very bravely and won his kingdom back.

Tapti, the daughter of Surya, the sun god, had seen the courage of Sarvan in the war and fell in love with him. She decided to find out whether Sarvan would be willing to take her as his bride.

After becoming a king again, Sarvan went hunting. He saw a beautiful deer in the forest and chased it. After some time the deer suddenly disappeared and a beautiful woman appeared before him. She glowed like gold. The moment he set his eyes on her he fell in love with her. He asked her who she was and she told him that she was Tapti, the daughter of Surya. Sarvan expressed his desire to marry her. Tapti said that he would have to seek the permission of her father. Sarvan started performing *tapasya* to please Surya. After twelve days, Vashishtha came to him and said that he himself would take his proposal to Surya.

Vashishtha met Surya who knew that Sarvan was a noble and worthy king. He immediately agreed to the match. Soon, Tapti and Sarvan were married in the presence of all the gods and sages.

# 18 Bhima and Bakasura

The Pandavas had decided to go into hiding for some time because the Kauravas were trying to kill them. During this time, they lived in a town called Ekchakra, with a Brahmin family.

One day, Kunti found her hosts crying and asked them the reason. The Brahmin said, "There lives a demon outside Ekchakra who once threatened to kill all the people of the town. To protect ourselves we made an agreement with him.

Every week one person would take a cartload of food to him. The demon eats the food as well as the person. All take turns to send one member every week. This week it is the turn of our family. I have to send someone to the demon." Kunti said, "I have fine sons; I will send Bhima to the demon. He is strong and will deal with him." Bhima took the food to the demon but started eating it himself. Seeing this, the ferocious demon attacked but the strong Bhima killed him with his bare hands.

## 19 Sita in Lanka

As Ravana entered Lanka with Sita in his flying chariot, people stood aghast.

He pulled her into his huge palace and showed her his royal chambers, his servants, and the vast army. Then he roared, "I'm the king of Lanka, the ruler of this land, its riches, and its people." Thinking that Sita would be impressed he offered her precious jewellery and gorgeous clothes. But Sita only repeated Rama's name.

Angry with Sita, Ravana told her that he would make her his queen. To this, Sita replied that the mighty Rama would kill him.

Leaving her under an Ashoka tree, Ravana said that if she did not accept his offer he would kill her.

Under the watchful eyes of a she-demon, Sita began passing her days thinking and chanting Rama's name.

## 20 Arjuna and Angarparna

When they were in hiding, the Pandavas came to the river Ganga one night. A warrior came riding in his chariot and shouted, "I am Angarparna, a heavenly being. This part of the forest belongs to me. You can't cross the river here." Arjuna said, "Sacred river Ganga is nobody's property." Angry Angarparna roared, "You have no idea how strong I am." Now Arjuna was also angry, he said, "You have never fought with a true warrior.

I challenge you to a fight." Hearing this, Angarparna attacked Arjuna with his sword. Arjuna escaped his blow and threw at him the burning *mashaal* (torch) that he held. It landed on Angarparna chariot and burnt it down. Angarparna jumped out of his chariot and fainted. When Angarparna came to his senses he begged for forgiveness. Forgiven by the Pandavas, he presented them with *chakshushi*, the divine sight by which they could see anything at any place and at any time.

## 21 Kabandha Meets Rama

In the forest, Rama and Laxmana saw a ferocious demon. His name was Kabandha.

The hungry demon caught hold of them and was about to eat them, when the brothers fired arrows and cut off his arms.

As Kabandha lay bleeding he asked them about their identity. When Rama and Laxmana introduced themselves, Kabandha bowed in reverence and told them his story. He said that Brahma had cursed him to change into a demon for his misdeeds and only if Rama

killed him could he get back his earlier form. Kabandha then begged Rama to end his life. As his body burnt to ashes a beautiful figure emerged from it. After changing into a *gandharva*, Kabandha advised Rama to seek Sugreeva's help and recover Sita.

## 22 Gajanana

Kubera, the god of wealth, once went to heaven where he met Shiva and Parvati. Parvati was so beautiful that Kubera kept looking at her. This made her very angry. Seeing Parvati angry, Kubera became fearful. From his fear emerged a demon called Lobhasura who went to the kingdom of demons. There he performed a long *tapasya*. Pleased, Shiva gave him the boon of fearlessness. After becoming fearless, Lobhasura conquered the

three worlds. He also went to Mount Kailash, the home of Shiva and threatened to conquer it. Shiva remembered the boon that he had given Lobhasura and left Kailash on his own. Tormented by the cruelty of Lobhasura, the gods went to Sage Raibhya who advised them to worship Ganesha. When the gods prayed to him, Ganesha appeared in his Gajanana form. Shiva went to Lobhasura and described the strength of Gajanana. Lobhasura became fearful and admitted defeat.

## 23 The Story of Shanti

An old lady named Shanti used to observe a fast on Tuesday, the day of Hanuman. Her daughter-in-law, Mala, treated her badly; she never gave her enough to eat. Every Tuesday, Mala gave Shanti four loaves of bread to offer to Hanuman. Shanti took these to the Hanuman temple, offered two to the god and broke her fast with the remaining bread. One Tuesday, Mala asked her children to follow Shanti. The children returned and told her that their grandmother ate two loaves herself. Mala became angry and the next time, gave Shanti only two loaves. Shanti offered one of them to Hanuman and ate the other. The children saw this and told their mother and the next time she gave Shanti only one loaf. Shanti offered half of it to Hanuman and ate the rest. When the children told her,

Mala became so angry that the next Tuesday she gave nothing to Shanti. Sadly, Shanti went to the temple. Hanuman appeared in the form of a small boy named Mangal and asked her, "Mother, why are you sad?" On hearing her story Mangal said, "I will build a hut and you can stay with me." Every day, Mangal gave Shanti milk and bread and took care of her.

When Shanti did not return, Mala was happy but soon poverty struck. She became poor. One day, she asked her children to look for Shanti. They found Shanti and told Mala that their grandmother was living comfortably. Mala realised that she had been unfair to her mother-in-law and as a punishment from god she had become poor. She went and apologised to Shanti. Mangal told Shanti to go with her as she had realised her mistake.

## 24 Bali and Sugreeva

Bali was the monkey king of Kishkindha. The son of Indra, his younger brother was Sugreeva. The kingdom had a sworn enemy called Mayavee. Tired of its attacks, Bali decided to settle the score. When Bali and Mayavee entered a cave during their fight, Sugreeva was ordered to keep a watch outside till Bali emerged.

Time passed and sounds of the roaring fight wafted to Sugreeva's ears. After nearly a year's wait when neither Bali

nor the *rakshasa* (demon) came out, Sugreeva thought they had both been killed. Saddened by his brother's death, he went back to Kishkindha and became its ruler and made Tara, Bali's wife, his queen.

However, Bali returned and seeing Sugreeva as king, Bali thought he had been betrayed. Though Sugreeva tried to explain the misunderstanding, Bali attacked and forced him and his team of monkeys to flee Kishkindha. Bali regained his kingship but became an enemy of Sugreeva forever.

# 25 The Brave Man

Vikram put Betal on his shoulders and started walking. Betal began another story.

A woodcutter named Mohan once saw a wolf attacking a girl in the forest. He saved her and killed the wolf. She was actually a princess. As a reward for his bravery, Mohan was made a soldier in the king's army. Once, in a battle he fought bravely and even saved the king's life. Mohan became famous for his courage. Then he got married and had children. One day, a gang of robbers entered the kingdom and started killing and robbing people. The king asked Mohan to fight the robbers but he refused. Betal said, "Tell me, Vikram, why did he refuse to fight the robbers? Had he lost his courage?" Vikram replied, "Mohan did not lose his courage, but now that he was a married man, he did not want to risk his life." Betal said, "You are right, but you opened your mouth, so here I go." Saying so, Betal flew away.

# 26 Krishna and Kesi

Kansa carried on with his attempts at killing Krishna.

Once he sent the demon Kesi, to kill Krishna. Kesi took the form of a terrible horse. He came galloping to Vrindavan with his mane flowing and hooves clattering.

After entering Vrindavan, Kesi challenged Krishna in a duel.

As Krishna accepted the challenge, Kesi dug up the earth with his hooves and charged towards him like an angry lion. With great might, he jumped on Krishna and tried to trample him with his hooves.

Krishna caught hold of his legs and after swinging him around, flung him on the ground. Kesi fell with a thud and became unconscious. After regaining his senses he again attacked, but this time Krishna put his hands into his mouth and choked him to death.

## 27 Shabri

Shabri was a tribal woman, who lived in a small hut in Sage Matang's ashram in the forest. She was a great devotee of Rama. Before he died, Sage Matang told her that her devotion would be rewarded and Rama would visit her one day. Many years passed by and Shabri grew old. Each day, she cleaned her hut and the surroundings and waited patiently for Rama to come and visit her. Finally, one day, Rama and Laxmana stopped by the ashram in their search for Sita, who had been kidnapped by Ravana. Shabri was overjoyed and took them to her hut. She washed their feet lovingly. She had collected berries for Rama. Shabri tasted each berry herself and offered him only the ones that were ripe and sweet. Laxmana was annoyed by this and threw the berries away in disgust. Rama then gently explained to Laxmana that tasting the berries before giving them to Rama to eat showed Shabri's love and devotion.

## 28 Krishna Kills Vyomasura

Vyomasura was the son of the demon Maya. He had acquired great magical powers. He had an evil eye and wanted to steal the cowherd friends of Krishna. One day, while Krishna and his friends were playing in the fields, Vyomasura disguised himself as another cowherd and appeared before them. One by one he started abducting Krishna's friends.

Seeing his men disappear, Krishna grew curious. Then, he spotted a cowherd who looked different from the rest. Krishna realised that something was amiss. He went up to the boy and grabbed his collar. Fearing an attack from Krishna, Vyomasura instantly changed himself into a big monster. As Vyomasura's size grew, Krishna grabbed his feet, lifted him up, and threw him to the ground with full force, and killed him.

## 29 The Honest Girl

Vikram put Betal on his shoulders. Betal started a new story. A king wanted his son to marry the princess of the neighbouring kingdom. He asked him to disguise himself as a merchant and find out if she loved someone else. The prince went to the kingdom and stayed at an inn, but he fell ill. The innkeeper's beautiful daughter looked after him. The prince fell in love with her. But he wanted to fulfil his task. He told her, "The prince of the neighbouring kingdom is my friend. He wants to marry the princess. Ask her if she loves someone else." When the innkeeper's daughter asked the princess, she said that she didn't love anyone else. The girl came to know that the merchant was really the prince. To marry the prince, she could have told him that the princess was in love with someone else, but she told him the truth. Betal said, "Vikram, did the prince marry the girl?" Vikram replied, "Yes, because she had been honest." Betal said, "That is the right answer, but you spoke, so here I go."

## 30 Krishna's Journey to Mathura

Kansa sent Akrura to fetch Krishna and Balarama from Gokul where Nanda, Yashoda, along with the people of Gokul, bade them a tearful goodbye.

As their chariot approached the banks of the Yamuna, Akrura decided to refresh himself. Suddenly, he saw the figures of Krishna and Balarama emerge from the deep waters. Seeing this, he was confused and looked at the chariot where he saw the brothers sleeping.

On looking back into the river, he saw a beautiful vision of Krishna, in the form of Lord Vishnu, sleeping on Sheshnag. After some time the curved body of the snake turned into the stunning form of Balarama.

Akrura was overjoyed, as he understood that Krishna and Balarama had shown him their true forms.

# 31 Venus

Once, a newlywed young man called Vinod went to his in-laws' house to pick his wife Seema and bring her back to his own house.

His in-laws were very superstitious and said that the planet Venus, the planet of love, was not in the sky and therefore, it was not a suitable time for the couple to start their married life. But Vinod was adamant. He thought that he knew best and refused to listen to their advice. Soon, he set off for home with his wife.

The journey was very long and tiring. Hardly had the couple left the town, than their bullock cart broke down and their bullocks got injured. They had no other option and continued their journey on foot. Further on, some robbers attacked them and stole all their money and Seema's precious ornaments. They somehow managed to save their lives and escape from the robbers.

Before they reached their destination, Vinod fell very ill and they couldn't continue on their journey home. When Vinod's parents came to know what had happened they asked him to return to his in-laws' house with Seema and come back with her when Venus rises.

Vinod realised his mistake; he did as his parents told him and went back to his in-laws' house and waited there for an oppurtune time to come back to his own house. Thereafter, Vinod and Seema lived a happy married life.

# Contents

*The Story of the Month:   Draupadi's Swayamvara*

The Story of the Month

# Draupadi's Swayamvara

## Draupadi's Swayamvara

Draupadi was the beautiful daughter of Drupada, the king of Panchala. Drupada arranged a *swayamvara* for Draupadi's marriage in the Panchala court. At the centre of the court a pole was erected over which there was a revolving wheel. On the wheel was a wooden fish. At the bottom of the pole there was a pan of water. The one, who could shoot an arrow at the *eye* of the revolving fish while looking at its reflection in the water below, would marry Draupadi. This was the condition for the *swayamvara*. Princes from all over assembled for the *swayamvara*. The Pandavas who were at that time living as Brahmins were also present. Duryodhana, Karna, and Shri Krishna were also present.

As the *swayamvara* began, many brave princes tried to win the hand of Draupadi, but failed to perform the difficult task of shooting the fish's *eye*. When Karna came forward to show his skill, Draupadi stopped him and said, "I will not marry a charioteer's son." Insulted, Karna left the court.

When all the princes were unsuccessful in performing the feat, Drupada became worried about the marriage of his daughter. Suddenly, Arjuna dressed as a Brahmin rose to try the feat. Nobody was able to recognise him. All the princes objected to the participation of a Brahmin in a competition that was meant for them. But looking at the build and confidence of the Brahmin, no one dared to say anything. Arjuna easily shot the fish's *eye*. Draupadi was very happy and she put the wedding garland around Arjuna's neck.

All the princes felt humiliated and were jealous of Arjuna. They attacked him. Bhima came to his rescue. The mighty Pandavas easily defeated all the princes and took Draupadi with them. Drhishtdyumna, Draupadi's

brother, followed them to find out who the Brahmin was. When they reached their hut, the Pandavas called out to their mother, Kunti, "Look, Mother, what we have brought." Kunti replied from inside the hut, "Share it among yourselves," thinking that they had brought food. When she saw the bride and was told that she was Arjuna's wife, Kunti was very unhappy at what she had said. As a custom, the Pandavas would have to obey every word that she had said—Draupadi would have to become the wife of all five brothers. Just then Krishna came

to their hut. He told Kunti, "In her previous life Draupadi had worshipped Shiva to get a husband with five qualities. But Shiva had given her a boon that in her next life she would marry five men each having one quality." On hearing this Kunti felt satisfied and Draupadi became the wife of all five Pandavas.

Drhishtadyumna who had followed them, heard all this. He went back to his father Drupada and said, "I have good news for you. The brave Brahmin who married Draupadi was none other than the

great Arjuna." Drupada was delighted to hear this. But when he came to know that Draupadi was to be the wife of all the five Pandavas, he was sad, because this was against the law. At that time, Sage Vyasa came there. He told Drupada, "Though such a marriage is not permitted in the Holy Scriptures, this particular marriage is a result of a boon by Shiva himself, so it is not against the law." Satisfied, Drupada arranged for a reception at the palace. The Pandavas were invited and the wedding between the Pandavas and Draupadi was performed with great splendour.

## 1 The King's Guilt

Vikram placed Betal on his shoulder and started walking. Betal began a story.

Once, a learned man, Shridutt, visited King Chandersen's court. The king was impressed by Shridutt's wisdom and intelligence. When Shridutt took his leave, the pleased king gave him a precious necklace. On his way home, a robber killed Shridutt and took the necklace away from him. The king's soldiers came to know about this and arrested the robber. The robber was hanged on the king's orders. But the king was very unhappy and blamed himself for Shridutt's death—had he not given Shridutt the necklace, he wouldn't have been killed. The king felt guilty and cursed himself all day. He could not eat or sleep properly and became ill. All

the royal doctors failed to cure him.

One day, the queen called for a doctor who was also a scholar. The doctor said that he had the power to bring Shridutt back to life. The king was happy to hear that but asked the doctor if he could bring the robber also back to life. The doctor said that through his powers he could bring only one person to life.

At this, the king said, "If you can't bring the robber to life then don't bring Shridutt to life either." Betal asked Vikram, "Why did the king say that?" Vikram replied, "The king thought that if Shridutt is alive, why should the robber be punished for his murder." Betal said, "You are right, but you broke your silence, so here I go." Saying so, Betal flew away.

## 2 Lopamudra and Agastya

Once Agastya, the great sage, went to heaven. There, he found his dead ancestors hanging upside down, which meant they would be going to hell. They said, "It was because of you that we are going to hell. You have not married and have no children who will continue our family. There will be no one to make prayer offerings on our behalf and therefore, we have to go to hell." Agastya said that he would go to earth and get

married. But no woman was worthy of marrying such a great sage.

At that time, the king of Vidarbha was performing *yajnas* for the birth of a child in his family. Agastya went and blessed him and eventually a daughter was born in the royal family. The king named her Lopamudra.

Lopamudra grew up to be a beautiful woman, worthy enough to be married to Agastya. Agastya married Lopamudra and saved his ancestors from going to hell.

## 3 Krishna in Mathura

Seated regally on the chariot, Krishna and Balarama entered the gates of Mathura.

The people of Mathura, tired of Kansa's torture, rushed towards the chariot to catch a glimpse of Krishna. They cheered and clapped as Krishna and Balarama smilingly waved at them. The brothers then went on a tour of the city where they met several people. First, they met a washerman. Krishna asked the washerman for some clothes, but he declined rudely, saying that they were Kansa's and could not be given to anyone.

Krishna then met a poor florist who took them to his house. When Krishna entered his house, the florist said he was blessed to have him as his guest. Krishna blessed him and granted him many worldly comforts.

## 4 Hanuman Befriends Rama

Following Kabandha's suggestion, Rama and Laxmana came to the Rishyamooka forest where Sugreeva lived with his army of monkeys. Thinking they might be Bali's spies, Sugreeva became worried. He ordered his loyal minister Hanuman to find out.

Hanuman took the form of a Brahmin and went to the brothers. Seeing Rama he knew that he could not be a wicked spy. At once changing into his original form he asked the brothers to introduce themselves. When Rama and Laxmana told him their story, Hanuman bowed respectfully and said he was Vayu's son and also the exiled king Sugreeva's deputy. On hearing that Rama and Laxmana had come searching for Sugreeva, Hanuman said it would be an honour to help Rama to free Sita from Ravana's clutches.

He promised Rama his eternal friendship, and then taking the brothers on his sturdy shoulders he flew to Rishyamooka forest.

## 5 The Reformation of Duraasadana

When Shiva and Parvati killed Bhasmasura the demon, his son Duraasadana was very angry. He performed a long *tapasya* and obtained the boon of immortality from Shiva. Scared by this, all the gods left heaven and hid in Kashi. Duraasadana followed them to Kashi and so they went to Kedarnath. There, the gods prayed to Parvati. An avatar of Ganesha, Vakratunda, with five faces and ten hands, came out of Parvati's face. She gave him a lion to ride. Vakratunda went and fought with Duraasadana. He assumed his huge form (*vishvaroop*) and placed his foot on Duraasadana's head to remove all his evil thoughts. Duraasadana was reformed and Vakratunda gave him the duty of removing evil, henceforth.

## 6 The Marriage of Kartikeya

King Nambirajan prayed to Shiva for a daughter. One day, while he was in the forest, he found a baby girl. He brought her up as his daughter and called her Valli. When she grew up, Kartikeya, the son of Shiva and Parvati, wanted to marry her. Kartikeya disguised himself as a bangle seller and went to her palace. He started talking to Valli. Valli's brothers who were very brave and strong saw this. They did not like their sister talking to a man. When Kartikeya saw Valli's angry brothers, he escaped by becoming a tree stump. Kartikeya went to Valli again, this time disguised as a tribal king, but when he saw her brothers he became a saint and escaped. Kartikeya wanted desperately to ask for Valli's hand in marriage. He asked his brother Ganesha to help him. One day when Valli was outdoors, Ganesha disguised himself as a wild elephant and attacked her. Kartikeya saved her life and then asked her to marry him. Valli gladly consented and they got married.

# 7 The Dreamer

Once again, Vikram picked up Betal and put him on his shoulder. Betal began a story. There was a rich man called Dhanilal. His relative, Chandu, lived with him. Chandu was young but lazy. One afternoon when he was sleeping, he dreamt that he was a rich man and Dhanilal his servant. In his sleep he spoke, "Dhanilal, you are my servant, come here." Dhanilal, who was nearby, heard this. He got very angry and threw Chandu out of his house. Chandu went to a sage and asked him to make him rich. The sage gave him a mantra and said, "Whenever you dream of something, if you want it to become true, chant this mantra." Chandu was happy; he went to sleep. He dreamt that Dhanilal was saying sorry and wanted Chandu to marry his daughter. Chandu woke and chanted the mantra.

At once, his dream came true. Chandu became Dhanilal's son-in-law and started living in his house. But the servants of the house did not respect him because he did not work. Dhanilal gave Chandu some money with which he started a business. One night he dreamt that he had become a rich businessman. He woke up and chanted the mantra. His business flourished and he earned a lot of wealth. But the other

businessmen did not respect him. One day Chandu dreamt that he had become king. When he woke he didn't chant the mantra. He went to the saint and gave back his boon. Betal asked, "Why did he do that?" Vikram replied, "Chandu had realised that without hard work he could earn money but not the respect of others." Betal said, "You are right, but you spoke, so here I go."

# 8 Krishna and the Washerman

While Krishna and Balarama were roaming in the city of Mathura they came upon a washerman cleaning his clothes.

Krishna asked him for some clothes and told him that he would be blessed for life.

Unfortunately, the washerman who was a servant of Kansa, did not understand Krishna's words. Instead he became very angry and said, "How dare you ask for clothes that belong to King Kansa." He warned the brothers that such

impudent behaviour could get them into trouble in Kansa's country.

To teach him a lesson Krishna lifted him and with a thrust of his hand severed his head, killing the washerman.

All the other washermen saw the power of Krishna. They understood that by killing their fellow washerman God was trying to pass on the message that one should be giving, and that God showers his blessings on those who give generously.

Krishna was then gifted a garment by each washerman.

## 9 Trayambakeshwar Jyotirling

Sage Gautama and his beautiful wife, Ahilya, lived in an ashram. The other sages' wives hated Ahilya. They asked their husbands to get Gautama and Ahilya to leave the ashram. The saints performed a *tapasya* to please Ganesha. When he appeared they asked him to help them get Gautama out. Ganesha became a cow and started grazing in Gautama's fields. Gautama hit the cow with a small stick. But even with a light blow, it died. All the sages called Gautama a sinner; they asked him to leave the ashram. Sadly, he left with his wife. He prayed to Shiva for forgiveness. Shiva appeared before him and told him the truth. At first, Gautama wanted to punish the sages for their misdeed, but he forgave them as it was because of them that he could see Shiva. He asked Shiva to stay there forever. Shiva consented, and became the Trayambakeshwar *Jyotirling*.

## 10 Krishna Breaks the Bow

Krishna and Balarama arrived at the venue where Kansa's famous sacrifice, the *dhanur yajna*, was to be held. There, an enormous bow was placed on a platform to display Kansa's power.

Seeing the bow, Krishna went ahead to pick it up but was stopped by the guards. A fight followed and the guards were beaten badly. Krishna then climbed on the platform, held the heavy bow in his hand and bent it. The bow broke with a thunderous sound, so loud that it even reached Kansa's ears, miles away in his chamber.

The sound was like a clear signal to Kansa that the eighth child of Devaki had finally arrived and that his end was near.

In desperation, Kansa even sent an army of men to capture Krishna but was again defeated after a severe battle.

## 11 Indra

Indra is the god of thunder and rain. Though displaced by Shiva and Vishnu among the primary gods, he still retains an important position and is often referred to as Devraj Indra. Indra is shown carrying the conch, hook, the sword, the noose, a rainbow, and the roaring thunderbolt or *vajra*. His *vahana* is the white elephant, Airawat. He lives on Mount Meru with his wife Indrani.

## 12 Karna's Plan

When Arjuna won Draupadi at the *swayamwara*, Duryodhana who had thought that he had killed the Pandavas in the lac palace, came to know that they were alive. He feared that Yudhisthira would come and claim the throne of Hastinapur. Karna who was the best friend of Duryodhana, told him about a plan to get rid of the Pandavas. The Pandavas were staying in the palace of Drupada, king of Panchala, so Karna suggested that Duryodhana take the army of Hastinapur and attack Panchala, and capture the Pandavas. Duryodhana was delighted and went to the elders of Hastinapur to seek their approval. Bhishma, Drona, and Vidura condemned the plan and warned Duryodhana against his evil designs. Although Dhritarashtra in his heart wanted Duryodhana to be king, he had to go along with the decision.

## 13 Sugreeva's Promise

When Hanuman reached Rishyamookha forest with Rama and Laxmana, all the monkeys came to see them. Hanuman introduced Rama and Laxmana to the entire army of monkeys. Sugreeva embraced them and welcomed them to the forest.

Hanuman began narrating Rama's problem and spoke of how Kabandha had advised them to seek Sugreeva's help.

Hearing of Rama's plight, Sugreeva showed him a handful of jewels. Recognising these as Sita's, Rama asked Sugreeva where he had found these. Sugreeva replied that one day he heard a lady screaming Rama's name while being carried away on a flying chariot. On her way she had scattered these jewels. Unable to see Rama's grief, Sugreeva, Hanuman, and all the monkeys promised their support in bringing back Sita from Lanka.

## 14 Devhuti

Manu and Satarupa had a daughter named Devhuti. She wanted to marry the legendary sage, Kardama. To fulfil their daughter's wish, Manu and Satarupa went to meet Kardama.

Kardama agreed to the proposal, but he lay a condition that as soon as Devhuti had a child, he would retire to the forests. Manu agreed and got them married. After some years Devhuti gave birth to nine daughters and Kardama got ready to leave. Devhuti pleaded with him saying that she wouldn't be able to shoulder the responsibility of bringing up her daughters alone.

Kardama assured her that if she drowned herself in God's worship he would help her. Devhuti began worshipping the lord and was granted a son named Kapil. Her daughters were married off, and under Kapil's guidance, Devhuti began her meditation on the banks of Saraswati. Completely lost in God, she attained salvation at the place, which is today known as Siddhipad.

## 15 Krishna Kills the Elephant

Once, Kansa decided to send his faithful elephant, Kuvalayapeeda, to fight Krishna and Balarama. Seeing Krishna, Kuvalayapeeda tore open his shackles and charged towards him. He climbed the stage where Krishna was standing, grabbed him with his trunk, and was about to throw him on the ground when Krishna slipped out of his grip and quickly hid behind his hind legs. Seeing Krishna slip out, Kuvalayapeeda raised his leg to crush him, but he again escaped unhurt. Seeing the ferocious elephant-demon, Balarama rushed to save his brother. Casting a cruel glance at the brothers, the elephant charged towards them with his huge tusks. Krishna and Balarama firmly grabbed each of his tusks and broke them into pieces. As the elephant fell on the ground, the brothers killed him with his own tusks.

## 16 The Mischief of Lord Mars

A couple was once travelling through a forest. When Mars saw the beautiful wife he felt like getting up to some mischief. He took the form of the husband and went to the couple. He asked the wife to go with him. The real husband became angry and they started fighting. Some villagers came to see what was going on, but nobody could tell who the real husband was.

One of the villagers realised that some heavenly spirit had taken the form of the husband. He brought an earthen pot with a spout and said, "Whoever can enter this pot through this spout is the real husband." At this the real husband said that it was an unfair test, he could never enter the pot. But Mars knew how to change the shape of his body. He made his body small and entered the pot through the spout. The villager closed the pot and Mars was trapped in it and the real husband took his wife with him.

---

## 17 Ajay and Malti

A young man named Ajay, once went to his in-laws' house to bring his wife, Malti. He insisted on leaving with Malti on a Wednesday. The in-laws tried to stop him saying that Mercury is not favourable for girls on a Wednesday but Ajay did not listen to their advice and took Malti with him.

On their way, Malti felt thirsty and asked him to bring water. While he was gone, Lord Mercury took the form of Ajay and came to Malti with water. Malti took him to be her husband. When Ajay arrived he was surprised to see his wife talking to another man who looked just like him. He asked Malti to come with him. Malti was very confused as to who was her real husband. The two men began fighting.

Hearing the noise, a soldier came to them. The soldier took them to the king to settle the matter. The king was also puzzled and ordered that they be locked up in separate cells in the prison while the guards kept a watch. In prison, Ajay remembered his in-laws' words and felt sorry that he had not respected Mercury. He was very disturbed and all night he did not sleep and prayed for forgiveness. Lord Mercury heard this and forgave him. In the morning the guards told the king that one of the men was restless and could not sleep at night. The king came to the conclusion that he was the real husband and sent Malti with him.

## 18 The Banana Tree Goddess

Once there was a little girl who watered a banana tree everyday. One day a voice came from the tree, "Will you play with me?" The girl was very scared and ran to her mother. Her mother said, "Don't be afraid, that voice is of the banana tree goddess, Laxmi. She is pleased with you." The next day when the girl went to the tree Laxmi played with her. Later, Laxmi said, "I live in this tree. Will you come to my house for lunch?" Then through the hollow of the tree she took her to a beautiful palace and gave her delicious food in utensils made of gold and silver.

When the little girl returned and told her mother what had happened, the mother was very happy and said, "Invite Laxmi to our home tomorrow for lunch." The girl said, "But mother, we are so poor and our hut is so small. All our utensils are broken and our clothes are old. How can I invite her here?" Her mother said, "Don't worry, she would be very happy with our love and courtesy." The next day the little girl brought Laxmi with her. As soon as Laxmi entered the small hut, it turned into a beautiful house. The utensils in which the food was served turned into gold utensils. Their old clothes became new. The girl's mother asked Laxmi to stay in the house with them forever.

Laxmi said that her blessings would be on their home as long as they worked hard and watered the banana tree. Saying so, she went back to the tree. The little girl watered the tree everyday and they lived happily ever after.

## 19 Bali and Dundubhi

When Rama told Sugreeva about Sita's kidnapping, he promised his allegiance to Rama. Sugreeva then narrated the story of his exile. He told him how he had been ousted by his brother, Bali and forced to live in the forest. Rama said it was his duty to help his friend, but Sugreeva said nobody could help him in his fight against Bali because by a boon that had been granted to him all Bali's enemies lost their strength before him.

Sugreeva then gave Rama a picture of Bali's might. When Dundubhi arrived to fight Bali, he was in his palace in Kishkindha. Dundubhi thought he would crush the monkey king easily, but he was proved wrong.

Bali accepted the challenge and, in the battlefield, lifted the enormous Dundubhi, then grabbing him by his horns, swirled him round and round till he lost consciousness. After this he swung his huge body with such strength that it fell miles away in the forests of Rishyamookha.

## 20 The Pandavas Get Half the Kingdom

After the marriage of the Pandavas, Vidura went to Panchala and told them, "Bhishma, Drona, King Dhritarashtra and Queen Gandhari, all want you to return to Hastinapur." But the Pandavas were not sure if they would be safe near Duryodhana. Krishna advised Vidura to divide Hastinapur between the Kauravas and Pandavas to ensure peace. The Pandavas went to Hastinapur and were given a warm welcome. Dhritarashtra told Yudhisthira, "The throne of Hastinapur belongs to you. But when your father Pandu died, you were very young so I was made king. Due to this, Duryodhana wants to be king. So everybody has decided to give you half the kingdom." Yudhisthira agreed and became the ruler of half the kingdom with its capital in Indraprastha.

## 21 Ganesha Writes the Mahabharata

Ved Vyasa was a great poet. He was instructed by Brahma to compose the world's greatest poem, the *Mahabharata*. Ved Vyasa told him that he needed someone to write it down while he composed it. Brahma asked him to pray to Ganesha, because only he could understand and write what Ved Vyasa would dictate. Ved Vyasa prayed to Ganesha. When Ganesha appeared, Ved Vyasa said, "Would you be able to write as fast as I dictate?"

Ganesha in turn challenged him, "Would you be able to dictate as fast as I write?" They made an agreement that once started, Ved Vyasa would not stop dictating and Ganesha would not stop writing and that he would only write what he understood. As they started the *Mahabharata*, whenever Ganesha wrote too fast, Ved Vyasa would dictate difficult verses. Ganesha would take time to understand them and in the meantime Ved Vyasa would compose more verses. Thus the great epic was written.

## 22 Brahma and Gayatri

Gayatri is a vedic hymn, which when recited takes away all our guilt and fear.

One day, Brahma was performing a crucial *yajna*, which in order to be complete required his wife, Saraswati's presence, but she was nowhere to be found. Furious with her for her absence, Brahma asked the priest to go and fetch any woman for him to marry.

The priest went out and found a beautiful shepherdess. She was none other than the same holy hymn of *gayatri*, which had transformed itself into a woman to help Brahma. Brahma married her and she became his second companion.

Gayatri is depicted as seated on a pink lotus. She has five heads, the first four representing the Vedas, while the last one represents Lord Brahma himself.

## 23 Curse on Bali

After Sugreeva recited the Dundubhi story, he showed Rama the demon's carcass, which lay nearby. He then told Rama the truth about making Rishyamookha his hiding spot.

He informed Rama that the famous sage Matang Muni lived in the Rishyamookha mountain. When Bali had swung the battered body of Dundubhi from Kishkindha, it fell inside his ashram. The sage had become enraged because he had built the ashram after years of wor-

ship and used to organise his *yajnas* here. Matang Muni roared, "Who dares to sully my ashram with a blood-smeared corpse?" When no answer came, he sat down in deep mediation and discovered the name Bali. In a fury, the sage cursed Bali and his men by saying that if ever they entered the forests of Rishyamookha they would be destroyed. Sugreeva thus added that because Bali would hunt him down wherever he went, he took shelter in these forests knowing that he could not enter it.

## 24 Krishna and Muchukunda

Muchukunda was born to the same Ikshavaku dynasty as King Rama. He was so powerful that even Indra would seek his help.

Once, unable to bear the onslaught of the demons, the gods came to him for protection. He became their commander and helped them win the battle, but in the process lost his family. Pleased at his service, the gods allowed him to ask for any boon.

Muchukunda who had not slept for several ages due to the prolonged fight, asked for a peaceful sleep. The gods granted his wish and he slept for many *yugas*, till the Dwapara *yuga* when Krishna arrived.

One day, while living in Mathura, Krishna was attacked by the demon Kalavayana. He wanted to get rid of the demon and ran to Muchukunda's cave. The arrogant demon thinking that he would be able to kill Krishna, also followed.

However, Krishna entered the cave and hid, after quickly covering the body of Muchukunda with the silken robe that he was wearing. When the demon entered he mistook the sleeping Muchukunda for Krishna and tugged at the robe.

Muchukunda woke up, startled. Looking around he saw the fierce Kalavaya standing before him and cast such a fiery gaze that the demon was burnt to ashes.

Then seeing the whole cave illuminated, he started searching for the source of the light and discovered Krishna standing at a distance. Muchukunda fell at his feet.

Krishna was pleased to see Muchukunda's devotion and asked him to seek any boon. Muchukunda asked to be able to live in service of God.

## 25 The Just King

Vikram pulled Betal down from the tamarind tree and started walking. Betal began a story. Once there was a prince who had two friends, Bansi and Gopi. Bansi was a soldier so he was appointed as the prince's guard. The three once happened to pass a forest. Suddenly a tiger attacked the prince, and Bansi saved his life. After some time, a leopard attacked the prince. This time, Gopi saved him because Bansi was walking ahead. When they returned, the prince told his father what had happened. The king rewarded Gopi but not Bansi. Betal asked Vikram, "Did the king act justly?" Vikram replied, "The king was just in his actions. He did not reward Bansi because saving the prince was his duty. In fact, he neglected his duty the second time. But Gopi deserved the reward for he did something that was not his duty to perform." Betal said, "You are right. But you spoke, so here I go."

## 26 Kansa Is Killed

Finally, Kansa decided to get Canura and Mustika, the famous wrestlers, to kill Krishna and Balarama. Thousands of people gathered to watch the brothers fight the powerful wrestlers. Krishna and Balarama appeared fragile before the stout wrestlers, but they pushed, punched, and twisted their bodies with such force that Canura and Mustika died on the spot within minutes.

As the crowds cheered, Kansa, in a fit of rage, ordered the two brothers to be driven out of the city. Hearing Kansa speak this way, Krishna became very angry. He turned to Kansa and ran towards him. Kansa drew a sword and attacked Krishna. Fighting empty-handed, Krishna grabbed Kansa's long hair and struck him with his mighty fist. Kansa at once fell and died. The crowds roared and celebrated as they saw the cruel king breathe his last.

## 27 Akrura Meets Dhritrashtra

Kunti, the mother of the Pandavas, was always worried about the welfare of her sons. She was afraid that the Kauravas would kill them. She prayed to Krishna to help her sons. Krishna sent his messenger, Akrura, to judge the situation in Hastinapur. When Akrura went to Hastinapur to meet King Dhritrashtra, he realised that he was partial towards his sons, the Kauravas, and wanted them to take over the throne. He also realised that Dhritrashtra always supported his sons in their attempts to kill the Pandavas. Akrura indirectly advised Dhritrashtra to keep away from his evil plans and to give the Pandavas the throne, as it was rightfully theirs. But Dhritrashtra refused to change himself. Akrura returned to Krishna and Balarama in Gokul. He told them about the situation in Hastinapur.

## 28 Rama Proves Himself

Hearing reports of Bali's might, Rama was eager to prove his strength to Sugreeva. He kicked Dundubhi's carcass so hard that it went flying. But Sugreeva was not impressed as the mere carcass helped to prove nothing about Rama's power. Rama then took his bow and arrow and with one shot slashed seven trees one after the other. Finally convinced, Sugreeva asked Rama to fight Bali.

## 29 Indra's Pride

Indra was once sitting in his court with the other gods, when Vrihaspati, his guru, appeared. All the gods stood up to pay respect to Vrihaspati but proud Indra remained seated. Vrihaspati felt insulted and left. Realising his mistake, Indra went to Vrihaspati's ashram to apologise. Vrihaspati saw him coming but he was too angry to meet him and so he disappeared. Disappointed, Indra returned. Vrishvarsha, a demon, came to know about the conflict between Indra and his guru. To take advantage of this situation, he attacked heaven. Without his guru's blessings, Indra could not defend his kingdom and lost it to Vrishavarsha. Indra went to Brahma for help. Brahma told him to make Sage Vishwaroopa his guru. Indra requested Vishwaroopa to become his guru. Vishwaroopa agreed and with his blessings, Indra won his kingdom back.

## 30 Narmada

King Pururva once asked a saint, "How can a person be cleansed of his sins and go to heaven without performing *yajnas?*" The sage said, "Only the river Narmada can do this, but she is in heaven and will have to be brought to earth."

Pururva performed a long penance to please Shiva. When Shiva appeared he requested him to bring Narmada to earth. Shiva asked Narmada to descend on earth. But Narmada needed a base from which she could emerge on earth.

Shiva asked the mountains as to who was capable of providing Narmada with a base. The Maikal range of mountains agreed to it. When Narmada came on earth, she flooded all the mountains and forests. She was asked to control her force. Then Pururva purified his ancestors' souls by cleansing himself in the waters of the Narmada.

# Contents

*The Story of the Month:   Satyavadi Harishchandra*

The Story of the Month

# Satyavadi Harishchandra

# Satyavadi Harishchandra

Once there was a great king named Harishchandra who never lied and always kept his promise. He was the ruler of Ayodhya. He ruled his kingdom wisely. His subjects were happy and prosperous. He was well-known for his truthfulness. The gods decided to test him. They asked Sage Vishwamitra to help them.

One day, Harishchandra went hunting in the forest. Suddenly, he heard the cries of a woman. As he went to help her, he entered the ashram of Vishwamitra. Vishwamitra was disturbed in his meditation and became angry. To cool his anger,

Harishchandra promised to donate his kingdom to Vishwamitra. Vishwamitra accepted his donation but also demanded *dakshina* (fees) to make the act of donation successful. Harishchandra, who had donated his whole kingdom, had nothing to give as *dakshina*. He asked Vishwamitra to wait for one month before he paid it.

A man true to his word, Harishchandra left his kingdom and went to Kashi along with his wife, Shaivya, and son, Rohitashwa. In Kashi, he could not earn anything. The period of one month was about to end.

His wife requested him to sell

her as a slave to get the money. Harishchandra sold Shaivya to a Brahmin. As she was about to leave with the Brahmin her son began to cry. Harishchandra requested the Brahmin to buy Rohitashwa also. The Brahmin agreed. But the money was not enough to pay the *dakshina* and so Harishchandra sold himself as a slave to a *chandala* (a person who works in a cremation ground). He paid Vishwamitra and started working in the cremation ground.

Shaivya worked as a servant in the Brahmin's house. One day, when Rohitashwa was plucking flowers for the Brahmin, a snake bit him and he died. Shaivya

took her son's body to the cremation ground. There she met Harishchandra. He was filled with grief to see his only son dead. To perform the cremation, he asked Shaivya to pay the tax. But Shaivya didn't have any money. Harishchandra, who was duty bound, could not cremate the body without the tax. Shaivya was a devoted wife and she did not want her husband to give up his duty. She said, "The only possession I have is this old sari that I am wearing. Please accept half of it as the tax." Harishchandra agreed to take the sari. They also decided to give up their lives on their son's cremation fire.

As Shaivya tore her sari, Vishnu himself appeared with all the other gods. The *chandala,* who was actually Yama, showed his real form and brought Rohitashwa back to life. Harishchandra and his family passed the test; they had demonstrated great virtue and righteousness. All the gods blessed them. Indra asked Harishchandra to go to heaven with him. But he refused saying that he could not go to heaven when his subjects were suffering without him. He asked Indra to take all his subjects to heaven. Indra said that it was not possible because people go to heaven or hell depending on their deeds. Harishchandra said that he would donate all his virtues to his subjects so that they could go to heaven and he would bear the consequences of their sins. Seeing Harishchandra's love for his subjects, the gods were very pleased. They took all the people of Ayodhya to heaven. Meanwhile, Vishwamitra brought new people to Ayodhya and made Rohitashwa the king.

## 1 The Pink Pearl

Once again, as Vikram put Betal on his shoulders, Betal began another story.

King Vijendra possessed a precious pearl. When he became old he wanted to divide all his property among his three sons. But he couldn't decide whom he should give the precious pearl to. He decided to test his sons. The king called them and asked them to leave the palace and live as common people for a year and then tell him what noble deeds they had done during that time. The one who proved to be the noblest, would get the pearl.

The sons obediently went away and returned after a year. The first son said, "I worked in a jeweller's shop. He came to trust me so much that one day he gave me a bag full of gems to take somewhere. I could have run away with the gems if I wanted but I honestly delivered them to the right place." The second son told him that he saved a child who was drowning. The youngest prince said, " I could not perform any noble deed, but when I was coming back I saw a man sleeping on a hill at a place from which he could fall down and die. I went to warn him but recognised him as my enemy. I woke him up anyway, and warned him." Betal asked Vikram, "Whom did the king give the pearl to?" Vikram replied, "The king gave it to his youngest son. The first son had shown honesty, the second bravery but in saving his enemy the youngest son had shown nobility."

Betal heard this and flew away as Vikram had spoken again.

## 2 Tilottama

Sunda and Upasunda were two demon brothers. They were cursed to die at each other's hands but they loved each other too much to inflict any pain on the other. Tired of the destruction they had caused on earth, Brahma approached Vishwakarma, the heavenly architect, to find a solution. They decided to create a woman so beautiful that nobody could take their eyes off her. Accordingly, Vishwakarma created the exquisitely beautiful Tilottama, seeing whom even Shiva could not remove his gaze. Brahma then instructed her to meet the demons. Tilottama appeared before the demons and seeing her, both brothers fell for her charms. They both wanted to marry her and thus, a fierce enmity followed. They took up arms against each other and died fighting. Unfortunately, Tilottama's charms kept captivating one and all. So Brahma gave a curse that nobody would be able to cast his eyes on her for too long.

## 3 Rama Confronts Bali

Before going to the battlefield Rama and Sugreeva chalked out a plan. It was decided that Rama would shoot Bali while Sugreeva was engaged in a fight with him. As Sugreeva approached Bali for the fight, Rama hid behind a tree. However, just as the tussle began and Rama aimed his arrow, he saw two identical monkeys. Unable to differentiate between Bali and Sugreeva, Rama held back his shot. Unfortunately, Sugreeva who was no match for Bali's strength, was badly beaten by him. He somehow managed to escape his brother's clutches and enter Rishyamookha where Bali could not enter. Sugreeva was upset with Rama as he thought Rama had not kept his word. Rama, begging for forgiveness, explained his plight and they thought of another plan.

## 4 Krishna Meets Yama

Vasudeva put Krishna and Balarama under Sandipani Muni's training. After their training was complete it was time to ask for *gurudakshina*, the offering to be made to the teacher. Sandipani Muni wanted to ask for something extraordinary so he consulted his wife. She asked for her drowned son's return.

When Sandipani asked for his *gurudakshina*, Krishna and Balarama immediately set out for the ocean. On reaching its shores, they enquired about the dead son. The sea god emerged and told them how Panchajana, a demon, had devoured the child.

On hearing this, Krishna plunged into the water and killed Panchajana. He tore open the belly of the demon but did not find the child.

Krishna then dragged Panchajana's body to Samyamani, the residence of Yama. Yama was happy to receive Krishna and returned the child. Sandipani Muni saw the true power of Krishna and blessed him.

## 5  Indra's Fight with Vritra

One of Indra's famous battles was with the demon Vritra.

Vritra took the form of a fearful monster and stole all the water in the world. As the water disappeared, life on earth itself became threatened, but only Indra could save the world from this disaster.

Upon hearing what had happened, Indra pledged his help and went charging like thunder towards Vritra's fortress. As the building came crashing down, Indra saw Vritra standing in a corner. They clashed, and after a long drawn out battle, Indra killed him. He tore open the demon's body from which once again, all the water flowed out.

As the water flowed out, Indra was hailed as the king of the world.

## 6  Worms in Rice

Once, there lived a great saint, named Vedanta Deshikar. He was very simple and had no love for wealth and comfort. He loved to live his life like a religious person, and devoted himself completely to God. Everybody praised him for his simplicity and virtuousness.

Each day, Deshikar went from door to door and begged for alms and food. There lived a man in the same town who respected Deshikar a lot and wanted to gift something expensive to him. But he knew very well that the sage would not accept anything.

One day, when the sage came begging at the man's door, he put a few gold coins in the rice that he put in Deshikar's begging bowl. Deshikar went home with the rice but when he saw the gold coins he told his wife, "There are worms in the rice." He carefully separated the rice from the coins and threw the coins away and then ate the rice.

# 7 Uddhava Visits Vrindavan

Though Kansa was dead, Krishna knew that he could not return to Vrindavan as he still had to protect Mathura from the attacks of Kansa's friends. One day, he called his cousin Uddhava, whose bodily features resembled his very much, and asked him to visit Vrindavan on his behalf. He realised that the people would be anxious about his well-being. He wanted to reassure them. Uddhava immediately set out for the journey.

On reaching Vrindavan, Uddhava found the houses brightly illuminated and the air filled with the sweet fragrance of incense. But there were hardly any people on the streets and the hustle and bustle of the shepherd boys was also missing. Uddhava was puzzled. When he reached Nanda's house he saw Yashoda weeping in a corner. He rushed to ask her the reason. A tearful Yashoda said that everyone was missing Krishna dearly. Everybody carried out their duties mechanically, and that the joy of life had gone from Vrindavan. Uddhava consoled Yashoda and told her that Krishna had specially asked him to visit them and give them the joyous news of Kansa's death. He assured her that both Krishna and Balarama were in good health.

The news of Uddhava's visit spread like wild fire. In a while, he was surrounded by all the *gopis*, cowherds, and other citizens of Vrindavan. All were amazed at his likeness to Krishna. Everyone was eager to know all about Krishna. Uddhava answered their queries patiently. Their eyes lit up as the people heard the thrilling tales of Mathura. But soon it was time to bid goodbye and Uddhava, after taking the blessings of all elders, sat on his chariot and set back for Mathura.

# 8 The Competition

This time Vikram caught Betal before he reached the tree. Betal began yet another story. Bhupati was a rich man who had a son named Chander. His servant Bhola had a son named Suraj. Chander was spoilt and did not do well in studies. Suraj worked hard and performed well. Bhola wanted to send Suraj for higher studies. For this he tried to borrow money from his master. But Bhupati refused to help him.

One day, Bhupati overheard a conversation between Chander and Suraj. Chander said, "Why do you want to go for higher studies. I will give you some money to start a business." Suraj replied, "I don't need money for anything else." Bhupati went home and gave Bhola the money. Betal asked Vikram, "What made Bhupati change his mind?" Vikram answered, "Bhupati realised that Chander was getting jealous of Suraj. If he sent Suraj for higher studies, Chander would work hard to compete with him." Betal said, "You are a genius," and flew away.

## 9  The Story of Ahilya

Once Sage Vishwamitra had approached King Dasaratha for help. Some demons had been troubling the sages and were not allowing them to carry out their *yajnas* in peace. King Dasaratha agreed and sent Rama and Laxmana with Sage Vishwamitra to Mithila to fight with the demons and help the sages.

One day, while accompanying Sage Vishwamitra to Janakpur for Sita's *swayamvar*, Rama and Laxmana came upon a deserted hut. They wondered who the hut belonged to. Recognising the place, Vishwamitra told them that the hut belonged to the sage, Gautama, and his wife, Ahilya.

Ahilya was a very pious woman but when she had seen Indra the first time, she had developed a liking for him. Gautama came to know of her feelings for Indra and in a fit of rage, he cursed Indra to lead the life of a eunuch while Ahilya was cursed to turn into a stone.

Vishwamitra knew that Rama could relieve Ahilya of the curse and begged Rama to do so. As Rama entered the ashram his feet touched the stone and it was transformed into a beautiful lady. Ahilya had come back to her own form. In a moment, the ashram too came alive with colourful flowers, green trees, and the twittering of birds.

Ahilya thanked Rama and Laxmana and offered them her warm hospitality. Meanwhile, Gautama also forgave Ahilya and returned to live with her in the ashram. He then blessed the two brothers and thanked Sage Vishwamitra for his intervention.

## 10  The Grand Fort

Krishna took Vishwakarma's (the architect) help to design a fort to keep his relatives safe during Jarasandha, the king of Magadha's attacks. A vast wall was erected within the ocean. It had well laid out roads, gardens, and the wish-fulfilling tree *kalpavriksha.* Each house had underground rooms stocked with food to survive the siege. The city was presented with the celestial *parijata* flower, Varuna's horse, and Kubera's knowledge of gaining wealth.

# 11 Arjuna and Ulupi

Arjuna had broken a promise and had to go to exile for twelve years. While he was in the forest, a beautiful woman saw him and fell in love with him. She was actually a snake, called Ulupi. She was the daughter of the king of snakes, Kauravya, and lived in the snake kingdom in *patal lok* (netherworld).

Next day, when Arjuna went to take a bath in the river, Ulupi took her snake form and caught hold of his leg and dragged him to *patal lok*. There, she took him to her palace and asked Arjuna to marry her. Arjuna agreed. They got married and had a son named Iravan. Then Arjuna wanted to go back to earth and Ulupi took him there. She also gave him a boon that no creature of water could defeat him.

# 12 Vishwamitra and Menaka

Once Sage Vishwamitra was performing a very difficult *tapasya*. Indra, the king of gods, was afraid that once completed, the *tapasya* would make Vishwamitra very powerful and he would even be able to conquer heaven. So Indra sent Menaka, a beautiful dancer of his court, to earth.

Meanwhile, Vishwamitra had performed all the rituals and was engaged in meditation, which would complete his *tapasya*. Menaka went to the forest where Vishwamitra sat with his *eyes* closed. She sang, danced, made garlands of fragrant flowers and put them around Vishwamitra's neck to attract his attention. All this disturbed Vishwamitra and he opened his *eyes*. His meditation was broken. When he saw the beauty of Menaka he wished to marry her. They got married and had a daughter.

Once Menaka's purpose on the earth was over, she went back to heaven, leaving behind a sad Vishwamitra.

# 13  Rama Kills Bali

Rama and Sugreeva worked on a second plan to kill Bali. They decided that this time Sugreeva would wear a garland to help Rama recognise Bali. Sugreeva then invited Bali for the second time. As the fight began, Rama shot his arrow at Bali's chest, but he did not die. This is because of a boon given by Indra according to which, any attack from the front would lose its force before Bali.

Rama then shot at his back and the mighty Bali came crashing to the ground.

Writhing in pain he realised the trap Sugreeva had laid for him and in his final moments asked Rama as to why he had agreed to help Sugreeva.

Rama replied that he had become too powerful and arrogant. Besides by making Tara his queen, he had committed a sin.

After Rama explained, Bali with folded hands begged for forgiveness and said he was blessed to have been killed by the noble Rama.

# 14  The Mountain Bows

There were two mountains, Vindhya and Meru. The sun used to go around Meru but not Vindhya. This made Vindhya jealous. He asked the sun to encircle him but was refused. In anger, Vindhya grew and touched the sky. He blocked the sun. The earth was plunged in darkness. Without sunlight, creatures started to die. The gods went to Sage Agastya for help. Agastya promised to help. Vindhya knew he could not defeat Agastya and so he decided to please him. When Agastya came to him, he bowed his head in respect and invited him to stay. Agastya said, "I have to go for some important work. Stay in this position till I return." Vindhya realised his mistake, but he could not disobey a sage and stayed bowed. Agastya never returned. Now the sun's rays reached the earth and all was well again.

## 15 Arjuna and the Crocodiles

When Arjuna was in exile, he once went to an ashram, where the sages told him, "There are five pools of water nearby, where we bathed. But now there is one crocodile in each. The crocodiles eat whoever goes to the pools." Arjuna had received a boon from Ulupi, the daughter of the king of snakes, that no creature of water could defeat him. Arjuna fearlessly went to one of the pools and pulled the crocodile to the shore. Immediately, it turned into a beautiful woman and said, "I am Varga, a fairy in Kubera's court. One day, I along with four other fairies, Saurabha, Samichi, Lata, and Budbuda tried to disturb a sage who was meditating. He cursed us to become crocodiles. He said that when a brave warrior pulled us out of water, the curse would end. You have freed me from the curse, please save my other friends also." Arjuna agreed. The five fairies thanked him.

## 16 Kalyani's Devotion

There was an old lady called Kalyani who worshipped Shukra and fasted on Fridays. She would bathe the idol of Shukra in holy water and offer it the best food. Once she wanted to go on a pilgrimage. She asked her daughter-in-law, Gauri, if she would take care of the idol in her absence. Gauri was not a religious woman, but she agreed, as she wanted to get rid of her mother-in-law for some days.

While Kalyani was gone, Gauri would not fast on Fridays. As a holy bath she would put some drops of water on the idol. Instead of offering good food she would place some leftover crumbs in front of the idol. After sometime she got fed up and threw away the idol. A neighbour found it and took it respectfully to her home. She worshipped it and started fasting on Fridays. Soon the neighbour became very rich. But wealth left Gauri's home. When Kalyani returned she asked Gauri about the idol. Gauri told her that she had thrown it away. Kalyani went looking for it in the neighbourhood. When she asked the rich lady about the idol, she said, "How could you throw it in garbage, you have no respect for god." Kalyani told her the truth. The rich lady returned the idol. Kalyani brought it home and started worshipping it. Soon prosperity returned to her home and Gauri realised her mistake.

## 17 Vaishno Devi and Bhairav Nath

Shridhar was a very devout devotee of Ma Vaishno Devi. Once Ma took the form of a girl. The girl asked him to organise a big feast for the devotees of Vaishno Devi. Shridhar agreed and went out to invite people. He also invited Bhairav Nath, a sage, who asked him how he would make the arrangements. Shridhar was lost in worry when the girl reappeared and told him that all the arrangements had been made.

On the day of the feast, three hundred and sixty people were invited and ate in his small hut. Bhairav Nath was surprised by the divine powers of the little girl and he followed her to the Trikuta hills. For nine months he kept searching for her everywhere but couldn't find her.

Then, one day he saw the girl producing water from a stone by shooting it swiftly with an arrow. On seeing Bhairav she entered a cave. Bhairav Nath quickly followed her into the cave. With a trident she opened a path on the other end of the cave and left the cave. But Bhairav adamantly continued to follow her.

Finally, she took her real form and cut off Bhairav Nath's head. Due to his powers, his headless body remained alive. He begged the goddess for forgiveness. She not only forgave him but also gave him a boon that the devotees who would come to worship her in her holy cave would visit his temple thereafter.

Later a temple was built at the place where Bhairav's head fell.

## 18 Arjuna and Subhadra

While in exile from Indraprastha, Arjuna stayed in Dwarka as a royal guest of Krishna. There, he fell in love with Krishna's sister, Subhadra. He asked Krishna's permission to marry her. Krishna said, "A brave warrior never begs for a lady's hand, he either wins it in a *swayamvar*, or carries the lady away forcibly." Arjuna got the hint. One day, when Subhadra had gone to a temple, he carried her away in a chariot. Subhadra's guards tried to stop him but failed. They returned and informed Balarama, Krishna's elder brother. Balarama got angry and prepared his army to fight Arjuna. But, he saw that Krishna was undisturbed even after he received the news of what Arjuna had done. Krishna told Balarama that it was a matter of pride that their sister had become the bride of the prince of Indraprastha. Balarama was now convinced; he brought back Arjuna and Subhadra and formally married them.

# 19 The Search for Sita

Having slain Bali, it was time to crown Sugreeva king of Kishkindha. On his coronation there were celebrations all around, but for Rama and Laxmana the days of grief had only begun.

Sugreeva became so absorbed in the revelry that he nearly forgot his promise to Rama. Hanuman reminded his master of his commitment and sent out generals to all corners to begin the search for Sita.

Dividing his men into groups led by his generals, Hanuman, Neela, Angad, and Jambavan, Sugreeva gave them a month's time to finish their search and come back with the news of Sita's whereabouts.

Having full faith in Hanuman, Rama gave his ring to him and said, "When you meet Sita give her the ring and say that you are my messenger."

# 20 Kamadeva

The god of love is called Kamadeva. He is shown as a handsome youth, carrying a sugarcane bow and five flower-tipped arrows. Spring helps him select these flowers. His *vahana* or vehicle is the parrot.

Surrounded by beautiful fairies he searches for young maidens, boys, and sages at whom he can shoot his arrows to arouse feelings of love. Unfortunately once this act greatly angered Shiva.

Tired of the demon Taraka's attacks the gods went to Shiva, who alone could create a fighter to tackle the demon. However, Shiva was in deep meditation and nobody had the courage to wake him. So the gods decided to approach Kamadeva.

Kamadeva used a special shaft and awoke Shiva, but in the process also stirred his anger. Shiva cast his fiery gaze on Kama and burnt him to ashes. Hearing the pleas of Rati, Kama's wife, Shiva restored him, but only as an emotion. This bodiless form of Kama is called Ananga.

## 21 Abhimanyu

Abhimanyu was the son of Arjuna and Subhadra. He was very skilled at archery and was the pride of the Pandavas. Even as a lad, Abhimanyu was very brave and strong.

Once, while Abhimanyu was in his mother's womb before he was born, he heard Arjuna telling Subhadra how to tackle warriors when they surround you in a *chakravyuh* or maze during a battle. Arjuna explained to Subhadra how to enter a *chakravyuh*, but he was called away before he could explain the way to get out of it.

Consequently, Abhimanyu was born with the knowledge of how to enter a *chakravyuh*, without knowing how to get out of it. When he grew up, he was married to Uttara, the daughter of King Virata.

## 22 The War between Fire and Rain

A Brahmin once came to Krishna and Arjuna and begged for food. They promised to give him whatever he wanted to eat. Then the Brahmin took on his true form; he was actually Agni the firegod. He wanted to eat the Khandava forest. But the king of snakes, Takshaka lived in that forest. Takshaka was a friend of Indra the rain god. So every time Agni tried to burn the forest, Indra brought rains and put out the fire.

Agni asked Krishna and Arjuna, "Keep your promise and help me eat the forest." Krishna and Arjuna needed good weapons for that. Agni gave Arjuna a quiver from which he could take out as many arrows as he wanted.

Agni then set the forest on fire. As soon as Indra saw this, he brought rains. But Arjuna shot thousands of arrows in the air and formed a cover on the forest to block the rain. Agni burnt the forest completely and satisfied his hunger.

## 23  Narada Muni's Monkey Face

Once Narada was so immersed in meditation that Indra grew suspicious. He sent Kamadeva to tempt him into breaking his meditation. A beautiful girl emerged from Kama's arrow and began tempting Narada, but in vain. Kamadeva accepted defeat. At this Narada said, "Go tell Indra that Shiva is not the only powerful one, I too have conquered all temptation." Narada then began bragging about his achievement. He went to Shiva and told him the story. Seeing him showing off like this, Shiva advised him not to say anything to Vishnu, but Narada did not take his advice. He boasted before Vishnu, but Vishnu only replied, "Be on guard." Narada's pride had blinded him so much that he could not read Vishnu's warning. On his way back he spotted a beautiful city and discovered

that a king by the name Sheelanidhi ruled there. When Narada visited the palace he was informed about the *swayamvara* of Sheelanidhi's daughter, Shrimati. Seeing Shrimati, Narada was captivated. He instantly recognised her as Laxmi's incarnation and realised that only a man as glorious as Visnhu could marry her. Wanting to marry her himself, Narada began planning how he could get Vishnu's

glory. He went to Vishnu and prayed for a face resembling Hari. Vishnu granted his wish. Unfortunately Narada did not know that Vishnu's other name, Hari, also meant a monkey. Thus Vishnu actually bestowed a monkey's face on Narada. Unaware of the monkey face, Narada asked for the princess's hand at the *swayamvara*. Everyone mocked and laughed at Narada and showed him his monkey face.

## 24  Arjuna and Mayasura

When Agni the fire god was burning Khandava forest, a demon called Mayasura, came running out of it. He went to Arjuna and begged him to save his life. Arjuna agreed and protected him from Agni. Mayasura was very happy. He said, "You have saved my life. How can I serve you? I am a great architect and build wonderful palaces of illusions." Arjuna said, "Then build a magnificent palace for Yudhisthira in our capital, Indraprastha."

Mayasura built a majestic palace. He built a grand assembly hall around a pool of water. The floor of the assembly hall was built with marble that looked just like water. It was studded with gems shaped like fish, and was at the same level as the pool at the center. The whole floor looked like a pool. The palace also had a wall that looked like a door and a door that looked like a wall. Yudhisthira was amazed to see the palace. The Pandavas were very pleased with Mayasura.

## 25 Suryamukhi and the Prince

Vikram carried Betal who began his story. There was a young princess called Suryamukhi who was very good at fighting with a sword. Her parents wanted her to get married. She made a condition that she would marry the man who could defeat her in a sword fight. Many princes tried but no one could defeat her. A prince disguised as a commoner watched these fights to learn the techniques used by Suryamukhi. One day, he came as a prince and a fight was held. Suryamukhi recognised him. He defeated Suryamukhi and asked her to marry him. But she refused saying that it was against the law. Betal asked Vikram, "Why did she say that?" Vikram replied, "The prince had learnt the techniques of fighting from Suryamukhi, so she was his teacher. The marriage of a teacher and student is against the law." Betal said, "Vikram, you are right, but you have spoken again," and he flew away.

## 26 Hanuman Crosses the Sea

With his sharp vision, Sampati, Jatayu's older brother spotted Sita . He informed the searching squad of monkeys about Sita's presence under the Ashoka tree in Lanka. The monkeys decided to immediately start for Lanka, but a problem arose. Who would fly across the huge sea?

Angad could only go a hundred miles, while Jambavan was too old. Finally, Jamabavan realised that only Hanuman, the son of Vayu had the capacity to fly across the ocean. The monkeys got together to remind Hanuman of his strengths. Hanuman offered his prayers and set off on the journey. He increased in size and with a great roar, leapt up to the skies. As his gigantic shadow fell on the waters of the ocean, nature rose to help him. The sun reduced its heat, the moon showered its bright light, and the wind helped him keep afloat.

# 27 Rukmini

Rukmini, an incarnation of Laxmi, was born to King Bhismaka of the Vidharbha kingdom.

She was very enchanting even as a little child and grew up to be a very beautiful maiden. Many princes coveted her hand in marriage. She was charmed by the stories she heard about Krishna and fell in love with him at a tender age. As she grew and legends of Krishna's heroic acts reached her ears, her love for the handsome prince only became stronger. She pined to meet him once.

Unfortunately, Rukmini's elder brother Rukmi was a dear friend of Kansa. Hearing of Kansa's death at the hands of Krishna, Rukmi grew furious. He knew about Rukmini's love for Krishna and influenced Bhismaka into believing that it would be wrong if his daughter were married to the killer of Kansa. Bhismaka believed him, and arranged for Rukmini's marriage to Shishupala, the king of Chedi and a dear friend of Rukmi.

# 28 Krishna Comes to Indraprastha

When Mayasura built the exotic city of Indraprastha, even the gods came to see it. Yudhisthira decided to hold his famous *rajasooya yajna* there. Invitations went out to all, including Krishna. Krishna, accompanied by his wives, arrived at the gates of Indraprastha. The roads were all lined with elephants spraying rose water. Vibrant flags and festoons adorned every wall of the city.

Streets were decorated with statues made of gold. The entire city was dotted with colourful flowers. White swans swam in pools decorated with water lilies. Lamps made of precious jewels hung in every house.

As Krishna entered the gates, dancing girls strew garlands on his path while bugles and drums played to welcome the guest.

## 29 Dhoomravarna

Dhoomravarna is Ganesha's eighth incarnation. Ahantasura, the demon of pride, had learnt the Ganesha mantra from the demon priest, Shukracharya. He chanted the mantra for a thousand years and Ganesha blessed him with the boon of being invincible. Ahantasura began spreading terror everywhere. The gods went to Shiva and Vishnu, and were asked to chant the Ganesha mantra.

Ganesha finally appeared as Dhoomravarna after a thousand years of prayers. He sent Narada to Ahantasura advising him to give up all his wrong deeds, but the demon did not agree. Angry at the demon's behaviour, Dhoomravarana threw his *Ugrapash*, the noose, and destroyed his entire army. Ahantasura ran to Shukracharya for help, who advised him to surrender. Ahantasura fell at Dhoomravarna's feet and prayed for forgiveness. Though he was forgiven, Ahanatsura was restricted to staying only in *patal lok (netherworld)*.

## 30 Kaveri

King Kavera performed *tapasya* because he wished to help people. Pleased with him, Shiva appeared and blessed him with a daughter who would fulfil his wish. He named her Kaveri and married her to Sage Agastya. A demon, named Shoorapadma, wanted to trouble people so he prevented rain from reaching the earth. Kaveri prayed to the gods to help the people. One day, Sage Agastya went to a lake for a bath. Since he could not leave Kaveri alone in the ashram, he turned her into water and put her in his *kamandala,* the utensil for carrying holy water. As he entered the lake, he left the *kamandala* on the bank. Meanwhile, Ganesha took the form of a crow and overturned the *kamandala*. The water was released and Kaveri became a river. She helped the suffering people by providing them with water.

# 31 Shakti's Curse

One day Sage Shakti, Sage Vashishtha's son, was going through a forest.

Suddenly, King Kalmashapada's chariot blocked his path. In those days, it was customary for everybody to give way to a sage, a blind man, a crippled person or an old woman. But Kalmashapada was vain and did not give way to Shakti. Instead Kalmashapada rudely ordered him, "Move to a side and make way for the chariot. Don't you see that I am the king of this region?" Shakti tried to explain, "I am a sage. It is the duty of a king to make way for a sage." But King Kalmashapada was very proud and refused to move. Instead, he lashed at the sage with a whip. At this, Shakti got angry and cursed the king to become a demon.

Sage Vishwamitra, who was passing by, saw this incident. He was a big enemy of Shakti's father, Sage Vashishtha and heard Shakti cursing the king. He asked another demon, Kinkara, to enter Kalmashapada's body. When the demon entered his body, Kalmashapada became evil and lost his sense of righteousness. He thought that his behaviour had changed because of the curse of Shakti, so he went to Shakti and said, "Your curse has made me a demon. Since you are responsible for this, I will take revenge on you and will eat you up." Saying this, Kalmashapada roared and killed Shakti and ate him. Later, he even killed Shakti's brothers.

# Contents

*The Story of the Month:   Garuda*

The Story of the Month
# Garuda

# Garuda

Sage Kashyapa had two wives—Kadru and Vinata. Though both were sisters, they were jealous of each other. Kashyapa offered each of them a boon. Kadru said, "Let thousand brave and radiant sons be born to me." Kashyapa granted her the boon. At this, Vinata became jealous and said, "Let such sons be born to me, who are braver and brighter than even my sister's sons." Kashyapa granted her the boon also.

After sometime Kadru gave birth to a thousand snakes. Vinata laid two eggs and waited for them to hatch. But even after five hundred years, when they did not hatch, she got impatient. Thinking that Kadru's boon had already been fulfilled, she broke open one of the eggs. The bird in the egg, which was still half formed, became angry with Vinata for her impatience and cursed her that she would become a slave. He also told her that after five hundred years his brother would emerge from the second egg and would free her from the slavery.

One day Vinata and Kadru were arguing. Vinata said the divine horse Uchaishravas was fully white in colour. Kadru said that his body was white but his tail was black. They decided to lay a bet on this issue. Whoever would win, would become the other's slave.

Kadru knew that the horse's tail was white and she would lose the bet, so she asked her sons to go and twist themselves around the tail so that it looked black. But the snakes did not want to be a part of this trick, so they were hesitant. Kadru was very angry at the disobedience of her sons and cursed that all of them would die in a *yajna* fire. When Kashyapa came to know about the curse on his sons, he went to Brahma for help. Brahma said, "The

snakes are poisonous and wicked, they deserve to die." After much pleading by Kashyapa, Brahma finally granted him that the snakes that were good would survive.

In the meantime, the snakes scared after hearing their mother's curse, decided to follow her orders. They went and entwined around the tail of the horse and made it look black. Vinata lost the bet and became Kadru's slave.

After five hundred years, a huge bird named Garuda emerged from the second egg. This bird was powerful and shone brightly.

He was even brighter than fire and his light blinded everyone. The gods requested him to reduce his light. But like his mother, he also had to become the slave of Kadru and her sons.

One day, Kadru ordered Garuda to find an island for her and her sons. Garuda flew with them on his back and found a beautiful island in the middle of the ocean. But Kadru and the snakes did not like the island. They asked Garuda to take them to another island. Garuda then took them to another island, but he was fed up of

being the servant of his step-mother and stepbrothers. He asked his mother, "Why do we have to live like slaves?" Vinata told him about the bet and how she became the slave of Kadru. After hearing the story, Garuda asked the snakes, "I want to free myself and my mother from your bondage. What should I do so that you will free us from your slavery." The snakes replied, "We want you to bring *amrit* or the divine drink for us that would make us immortal. Then we will free you and your mother."

Garuda stole the *amrit* from the gods and rescued his mother.

# 1 The Real Husband

As Vikram carried Betal, Betal began another story.

Inder and his wife Indu were very religious. Once Indu's brother Sunder visited them. All three went to goddess Durga's temple. First Sunder entered the temple. On seeing the idol of Durga he was so overcome by devotion that he decided to sacrifice himself. He cut his head off in front of the idol. Then Inder entered the temple and saw his brother-in-law's dead body. He was also gripped by a sense of self-sacrifice and cut his head off. Finally, Indu entered the temple and saw the two dead bodies. She became very sad. She wept aloud and prayed to Durga to give her the same husband and brother in her next life.

As Indu prepared to give up her life, Durga appeared and

said that she was pleased with their devotion and would bring the two men back to life. Then she asked Indu to join the two heads with the respective bodies. When Durga put life into the bodies, Indu realised that she had mixed up the heads. Now, Inder's body had Sunder's head and Sunder's body had Inder's head. Betal asked Vikram, "Who was Indu's real husband?"

Vikram replied, "The head is the most important part of the body. A person has all his thoughts and memories in his head. The man with Inder's head had all the memories of Indu as a wife. So he was her real husband."

Betal was very happy to hear Vikram's answer but he flew away saying that Vikram had broken his promise by speaking.

---

# 2 Rukmini Sends a Message to Krishna

Rukmini was the daughter of the king of Vidharbha, Bhishmaka. She wanted to marry only Krishna. She overheard her brother and father discussing her marriage to Shishupal.

She rushed to her chamber and sat down to write a letter. In that she narrated in detail her feelings about him. She wrote how after hearing tales of his heroism she had fallen in love with Krishna. She described that her love was so deep that it would be meaningless to live

without him. Rukmini further wrote how her brother Rukmi was forcing her to marry Shishupal. Finally she ended her letter informing him about her plan to visit the Parvati temple on the day of her marriage and appealed to Krishna to kidnap her from there.

Rukmini's trusted servant was an old Brahmin named Sunanda. She called for him and urged him to rush to Dwarka with the letter.

Bowing respectfully Sunanda took leave and raced his chariot to Dwarka.

# 3 Hanuman Meets Surasa

Hanuman was on his way to Lanka when a hungry monster arose from the ocean. It opened its mouth wide and asked Hanuman to enter it. Hanuman pleaded with it to let him go, but the monster refused to listen.

Seeing no other way out, Hanuman first grew in size. When the monster too opened its mouth wide, he quickly shrank again and flew in and out of the monster's mouth. He said, " I have fulfilled your wish, now let me complete my mission."

This monster was actually the snake maiden, Surasa. Hearing Hanuman's plea she changed into her original form and replied, "My son, I'm Surasa, the snake maiden. The gods had sent me to test you. Go ahead, your mission will be successful."

Overcoming many more dangers on the way, Hanuman continued on his way.

# 4 Ma Vaishno Devi

Kali, Laxmi, and Saraswati combined all their strengths and created a beautiful girl who was to merge with Vishnu after acquiring spiritual enlightenment on earth. She was born as Vaishnavi. Her father advised her to begin her quest for gaining even more divine strength. She went to the forest to meditate. Vaishnavi was elated to discover that Vishnu had appeared as Rama on earth. She met him on his way to Lanka, and requested him to accept her. Rama promised but only if she recognised him the next time he arrived at her hermitage. The next time Rama appeared as an old man. Vaishnavi failed to recognize him. Rama urged her to go north and immerse herself in more meditation. Once, disturbed in her meditation, Vaishnavi transformed herself into a ten-handed goddess with a trident in one hand riding a tiger and beheaded the person. Tired of the many obstacles she ultimately changed herself into three rocks.

# 5 Rudraksha

A demon named Tripura performed a long and difficult *tapasya* and was granted a boon by Brahma. This boon made him very powerful and he conquered heaven. When the gods were driven out of heaven, they were helpless and went to Brahma for help. Brahma did not know how to solve the problem and sent them to Shiva. Shiva decided to help the gods and went to fight with Tripura. He killed him with an arrow. But while he was fighting a few drops of perspiration from his body fell on earth. Rudraksha plants grew in the places where the drops fell.

The seed of the rudraksha plant has a lot of religious significance. It is believed that counting the rudraksha beads while chanting Shiva's mantra cleanses a person of sin.

# 6 Krishna Kidnaps Rukmini

Krishna had heard stories about the princess of Vidharbha, Rukmini's character, virtue, and beauty. Once he received Rukmini's letter asking him to rescue her from marrying Shishupal, it only helped him to be more determined to marry her. Knowing that the task would not be easy he arranged an entire army. Fearing an attack from Jarasandha, Shishupal's friend, he urged Balarama to follow with his men.

On the way when Jarasandha's men attacked, Balarama countered the attack with his army. Krishna escaped even as Balarama fought on. Meanwhile Rukmini who was waiting at the temple grew anxious seeing the delay. She thought Krishna had not agreed to her plea. She was about to leave when she felt a heavy hand on her shoulder. She turned and saw Krishna standing before her. Overjoyed at the union, the lovers drove away on the chariot.

# 7 Bhima and Jarasandha

Krishna once approached Yudhisthira and said, "King Jarasandha is a very cruel king. He has received many boons from Shiva. He has defeated many kings and imprisoned them. He wants to imprison more kings so that when the number reaches one hundred and one he can sacrifice them to Rudra (a form of Shiva). We need to kill Jarasandha because sooner or later he will attack us. But he can only be killed by tearing his body into two parts." Yudhisthira asked Krishna, "Why can he be killed only in that way?" Krishna replied, "There is a story behind his birth. His father King Brihadratha had two queens, but was childless. He requested a sage to bless him with a child. The sage gave him a mango for one of his wives. But by mistake

Jarasandha's wives ate one half of the mango each and gave birth to two half-babies. These half-babies were joined to form one baby who was named Jarasandha. I will take Arjuna and Bhima with me to kill him." Krishna, Arjuna, and Bhima went to Jarasandha's palace and Bhima challenged Jarasandha to a wrestling fight. They fought for thirteen days. On the fourteenth day, Krishna encouraged Bhima to tear

Jarasandha's body apart. He demonstrated it by tearing a leaf in front of him. Bhima tore Jarasandha into two parts but both the parts moved towards each other and joined again. Jarasandha got up again to fight. This time Krishna asked him to throw the two parts of his body in opposite directions. Bhima again tore Jarasandha's body and this time threw the two parts in opposite directions so that they could not meet.

# 8 The Story of Brains Over Beauty

As Vikram lifted Betal, Betal started narrating another story. A merchant had two sons, Sudhakar and Dayakar. While Sudhakar was handsome, Dayakar was intelligent. After their father's death the business went to Dayakar. One day, a rich man came with the proposal of getting his daughters married. Sudhakar married one daughter, but the other refused to marry Dayakar. Dayakar vowed to marry a more beautiful girl.

Sudhakar wrongfully acquired

the property and Dayakar promised to return only after becoming richer. One day, he saved a rich merchant and his servant from robbers. Pleased, the merchant offered him employment. The merchant had an ugly daughter who used to be ill-treated while everybody liked his helper's beautiful daughter. Both wanted to marry Dayakar.

Betal asked Vikram, "Which girl did Dayakar choose?" Vikram replied, "The merchant's daughter, because she needed better treatment."

## 9 Krishna and Rukmi

Krishna had made a plan and abducted Rukmini and sped away with her in his chariot towards Dwarka. Soon the news of Rukmini's abduction reached her brother Rukmi's ears. He was furious and rallied his soldiers together and made preparations to fight with Krishna. He asked his men to stop the armies of Balarama while he met Krishna to slay him.

Rukmi raced his horse in the direction of Krishna's speeding chariot. Spotting Krishna and Balarama, he fired one arrow after another, but they failed to even make a dent on Krishna's steely armour.

Krishna then charged his arrows at Rukmi's horse, killing it and then destroying his chariot. Rukmi came crashing to the ground. Enraged, Rukmi picked up his sword to attack Krishna but Krishna shot an arrow, which split Rukmi's sword into two. Rukmi was helpless.

Krishna then took out his sword and was about to slay Rukmi when Rukmini came in between. She fell on Krishna's feet and begged him to spare her brother's life.

Krishna loved Rukmini very much and couldn't see her in tears. Hearing her plea, he spared Rukmi's life, but did not want to let him off without punishing him for his deeds. Krishna chopped off half his hair and a part of his moustache, which was considered to be the worst form of insult to a brave soldier in those days.

Krishna then returned to Dwarka with Rukmini and married her in a grand ceremony.

## 10 Hanuman Meets Sinhikaa

As Hanuman neared Lanka, he came across a place created by Brahma to form a shade over the universe. Here Indra's elephant Airawat, *yakshas*, *gandharvas*, and many other animals, lived.

When Hanuman crossed over a stream in this land, he suddenly felt all his powers disappearing. Puzzled, he looked down. He saw the powerful flesh-eating she-demon Sinhikaa. The she-demon started pulling his shadow, thus forcing him to lose his power and descend.

When she opened her mouth to eat Hanuman, he cleverly expanded himself as big as the sky. However, just as Sinhikaa expanded her mouth further to gobble Hanuman up, he shrunk himself and quickly went inside her mouth. There he pulled out her teeth, clawed her tongue, and then crushed her jaws.

As Sinhika fell into the water, the gods were pleased and showered flowers on Hanuman.

## 11 Hanuman Meets Lankini

After crossing the sea and killing the she-demon, Sinhikaa, Hanuman decided to enter the heavily guarded city of Lanka to search for Sita.

However, a very powerful demon by the name of Lankini always guarded the city. When she saw Hanuman approaching the gates of the city, she stopped him. Hanuman insisted on going in but she punched him and Hanuman punched her back.

Lankini was surprised at the monkey's strength and looked at him closely with a puzzled look on her face. At once, she recognised him. She said, "Brahma had predicted that the day a monkey hits you, know that Ravana and all the other demons would be killed."

She set Hanuman free and allowed him to enter Lanka.

## 12 Naageshwara

Once there was a man named Supriya, who was a dedicated devotee of Shiva. He worshipped Shiva day and night.

Daruk, a cruel demon who lived nearby, did not like Supriya's devotion. In some way or the other, he wanted to hurt Supriya and was always thinking of devious ways of doing so. One day, he went with the other demons and captured the boat in which Supriya was travelling. But

Supriya was not affected by this. He made a *Shivalinga* on the boat and started worshipping it. When Daruk saw this, he ordered the other demons to kill all the people on the boat.

All of a sudden, Shiva appeared and killed the demons. Shiva then gave Supriya a divine weapon, the pashupatastra, with which he killed Daruk.

The *Shivalinga* which Supriya had made is still present in Dwarkapuri, Gujarat and is worshipped as Naageshwara.

## 13 Krishna Kills Shishupal

Seething with anger at Rukmini's marriage to Krishna, Shishupal wanted revenge. He approached Rukmi with the hope of getting his support, but Rukmi refused to help him after his humiliating defeat at the hands of Krishna and Balarama.

After Bhima killed Jarasandha, Yudhishthira organised a famous *rajasooya yajana*. He invited many kings and princes. Shishupal too was invited. As the *yajna* be-gan, Shishupal saw Krishna in the crowd. Seeing him there he began hurling abuses at Krishna. By insulting Krishna, Shishupal thought he would get the sympathy of the other guests.

The invitees stood startled but Krishna remained quiet. Finally, when Shishupal uttered his hundredth abuse, Krishna turned to him. Then taking his *Sudarshan Chakra,* he flung it at Shishupal. The weapon slashed Shishupal's head. As Shishupal lay dead, the crowds cheered.

## 14 The Imperial Yajna

Once Narada visited Yudhisthira and said, "Your father, Pandu, who is in heaven, wants you to perform the imperial *yajna* after which you will become *samrata* (emperor)." Yudhisthira asked Sage Vyasa to guide him. Vyasa sent the rest of the Pandavas in different directions to conquer the king-doms that were ruled by the Pandavas' enemies. They came back after bravely defeat-ing their enemies and brought a lot of wealth that could be used for the *yajna*. Yudhisthira invited many guests including sages and kings. Krishna also graced the occasion with his presence. Sage Dhaumya was made the royal priest for the *yajna*. Yudhisthira performed all the rituals. Offerings were made to the gods. Brahmins were given gifts and the *yajna* was completed successfully. All the elders blessed Yudhisthira and he became the *samrata*.

## 15 Sita and the Rakshasis

As time flew by, Ravana once again sent his fierce *rakshasis* to warn Sita.

The *rakshasis* came one by one and stood before her. She saw their messy hair, protruding teeth and sharp claws. Some had hunchbacks, while others, twisted arms. They laughed and mocked as Sita looked at them helplessly.

Sita wept pitifully when they tried to threaten her. As night drew closer more and more demons gathered around her.

When morning approached, Ravana accompanied by many other demons came to the Ashoka tree. He once again expressed his love for Sita and proposed to marry her.

Sita replied that Rama would kill him for committing these sins. Being ignored thus, Ravana said, "This is my last warning, if you do not accept this proposal, my cooks will cut you into pieces and feed the *rakshasis*." Saying these angry words Ravana left the place.

Sita closed her eyes and prayed to Rama.

## 16 Duryodhana Is Fooled

After Yudhishthira's imperial *yajna*, Duryodhana did not leave Indraprastha and stayed in the Pandavas' palace. He was amazed to see the wonderful illusions in the palace built by Mayasura.

When Duryodhana tried to enter a door, he hurt his head because it was not really a door but a wall. When he went further he saw a pool of water and tried to enter it. It was not a pool but glass which looked like a pool. He hurt his foot with the glass. Bhima and the other Pandavas who were present there were amused and made fun of him when they saw this.

Then Duryodhana went ahead but fell in a pool, which looked just like the floor. Seeing this, Draupadi, the Pandavas' wife, started laughing loudly. She commented, "A blind man's son is also blind." This rude comment insulted Duryodhana so much that he vowed to take revenge on Draupadi. Duryodhana became very jealous of the luxury of the Pandavas' palace. He said to his uncle, Shakuni, "I want to rob the Pandavas of all the luxury that they are enjoying. I want it all for myself." Shakuni said, "You can't take all this by force. We will have to make a plan to take all this from them."

Duryodhana agreed with his uncle and together, they started thinking of devious plans to oust the Pandavas from Indraprastha.

# 17 The Game of Dice

Duryodhana was jealous of the prosperity of the Pandavas and wanted to rob them of their wealth. His uncle, Shakuni, made a plan.

Yudhisthira loved gambling. They would invite Yudhisthira to Hastinapur for a game of dice. Shakuni was a master of the game and would throw the dice on behalf of Duryodhana and defeat Yudhisthira and win over his kingdom. Duryodhana liked this plan and asked his father Dhritarashtra to invite Yudhisthira. When Dhritarashtra hesitated, Duryodhana told him about the way Draupadi had insulted him and called him a blind man's son. Dhritarashtra gave his consent. Yudhishthira came with his brothers to the game. Shakuni used a charmed dice and defeated Yudhisthira again and again. Yudhisthira lost his palace, army, and the whole kingdom. Duryodhana was not satisfied at that, he encouraged Yudhisthira to stake his brothers. One by one, Yudhisthira lost all four of his brothers and then even himself. Duryodhana's joy knew no bounds.

When Yudhisthira lost everything he had, Duryodhana said, "Why don't you stake something else, maybe this time you will win and get everything back?" Yudhisthira said, "I have nothing left to stake." At this Duryodhana said, "Why, you have Draupadi, stake her." Yudhisthira was embarrassed by his defeat; he wanted to win everything back. He took his last chance and staked Draupadi. But he even lost her. Everybody was aghast at this turn of events. The Kauravas were jubilant.

# 18 Radha

Among all the *gopis* in Vrindavan, Radha was Krishna's favourite. She was the daughter of a cowherd Vrishabhanu and Kamalavati of Barsana.

Radha loved Krishna deeply and was very devoted to him. Often found singing and dancing together, their deep affection for each other made the other *gopis* jealous. When Krishna and his friends went to Barsana to smear colour on Radha, her friends beat them up with *lathis* or sticks and chased the boys away. This playful tradition is celebrated as *laathimar holi* in Barsana even today.

When Krishna left for Mathura and later became king of Dwarka, Radha waited earnestly for his return. Krishna had told Radha that her name would always be taken before his and that is why we always say Radhakrishna and never Krishnaradha.

Radha's birth is celebrated on Radha Ashtami, fifteen days after the birthday of Krishna.

## 19 The Miracle

When Duryodhana won Draupadi in the dice game, he asked his brother Dushasana to bring Draupadi. Dushasana grabbed Draupadi by her hair and dragged her to the court. Draupadi appealed to everyone, "I am the honour of this family. Why is everybody sitting and watching me being disgraced? When Yudhisthira had lost himself in the game, did he have any right to stake me?" The Pandavas could not do anything, as they were now servants of Duryodhana. Karna asked Dushasana to strip Draupadi of her clothes. Dushasana caught hold of one end of her sari and started pulling it. Helpless, Draupadi prayed to Krishna. To everyone's amazement, Dushasana kept pulling the sari but it would not end. In this way Krishna saved the honour of his devotee.

## 20 Trijaata's Dream

Ravana kept Sita a prisoner, in a garden, in Lanka. Among the *rakshasis* guarding her was an old and wise *rakshasi* named Trijaata.

One day, she said to the other *rakshasis*, "Leave Sita alone, for I have seen a bad dream." Trijaata told them that she saw Rama and Laxmana riding towards Lanka on their *pushpak vimaan* with Ravana's body hanging from it. She said that Ravana was dressed in a black robe and drinking oil. Sometimes laughing and sometimes crying, Ravana seemed to have gone mad.

She said that she also saw Ravana's sons and all the *rakshasis* going southwards riding on pigs while Vibhishana, dressed in a white robe, was the only one flying safely across the skies. Trijaata added that she later dreamt Rama, Laxmana, and Sita shining bright as the sun going northwards on a four-tusked elephant. Finally, as the gods rejoiced, Lanka sank into the sea.

# 21 Ganesha and Ravana

Ravana was a devout devotee of Shiva. Pleased with his worship Shiva handed over his *atmalinga* to Ravana, but at the same time, he warned him that the *linga* would lose its power if kept on the ground.

When the gods heard this they begged Shiva to take it back. But Shiva said that he could not do so. The gods decided to ask Ganesha to help.

Changing himself into a cowherd, he appeared before Ravana, who was then pondering how to take a bath with the *linga* in hand. He asked the boy to hold it for a while. The moment Ravana turned his back, Ganesha dropped the *linga* saying it was too heavy.

Furious, Ravana tried to lift it but failed.

# 22 The Story of Saturday

Laxmi and Daridra were sisters. While Laxmi was hardworking, Daridra was lazy. Pleased with Laxmi's virtues, Krishna married Laxmi. Laxmi asked Krishna to find a suitable husband for Daridra. Krishna said, "Nobody would like to marry her because of her laziness." Laxmi said a sage would be a suitable husband for Daridra as he would be busy in his meditation all day and would not be bothered by her laziness. Krishna found a sage who was ready to marry Daridra. But after the marriage, the sage was so fed up with her laziness, that he asked her to leave. Sadly, Daridra went to Laxmi and Krishna. Laxmi asked Krishna to find a suitable home for Daridra. Krishna found a peepal tree and asked Daridra to stay under it. Daridra asked Laxmi and Krishna to visit her, as she would get lonely. They promised to visit her on Saturdays. This is why people worship peepal trees on Saturdays because Krishna and Laxmi reside in them.

# 23 Pradyumna

One day, Narada appeared before Rukmini and told her that an incarnation of Kama, who was burnt by Shiva's gaze, would be born to her. Soon, Rukmini gave birth to a son. He was named Pradyumna.

Meanwhile, a terrible demon called Sambara was cursed to die by Pradyumna. As soon as the demon came to know of Pradyumna's birth, he took the shape of a woman. Sambara kidnapped the baby when he was just six days old, and threw him into the ocean. A big fish swallowed the child but Pradyumna managed to stay alive inside the fish. Meanwhile, Narada appeared before Sambara's maid, Mayavati, and informed her about the divine child. Mayavati was the reincarnation of Kama's wife Rati,

and she was earnestly waiting for his return. Overjoyed by Narada's information, she recovered the baby from the fish and took him under her care.

Pradyumna grew up to be a handsome young man and resembled Kama. One day, Mayavati told him the story of his birth and Sambara. Hearing all this, Pradyumna grew furious and vowed to take revenge.

Mayavati had great magical powers. She empowered Pradyumna with great strength to fight the mighty demon. Having gained the power, Pradyumna challenged Sambara to a duel. Eventually, he killed him after a long drawn-out fight.

Finally, Pradyumna returned to Dwarka accompanied by Mayavati. Upon reaching there, everybody, including Rukmini, came out to see the

divine Pradyumna. Krishna, who knew everything, invited Narada to narrate his story. After hearing his tale, Rukmini embraced her long-lost child.

Recognising them as incarnations of Kama and Rati, Krishna got them married in a grand ceremony.

# 24 Jagannath

At the end of *Dwapar Yuga*, Krishna realised that his end was near. He went to a forest and started meditating. When a hunter saw Krishna's foot from behind some bushes, he thought that it was a deer and shot a poisonous arrow at it. Krishna died and was cremated.

Vishnu appeared in the dream of King Indradyumna and asked him to build a temple for Krishna's ashes. When he woke up, Indradyumna

requested the divine artisan Vishvakarma to create an idol for the temple. Vishvakarma agreed on the condition that while he made the idol no one should disturb him. He locked himself up in a room and started work. After many days, when Vishvakarma did not come out, Indradyumna got impatient and broke down the door. Vishvakarma got angry and disappeared leaving the half-finished idol of Jagganath behind him. Indradyumna had a beautiful temple built in Puri where the incomplete idol was placed.

## 25 Pandavas in Exile

King Dhritarashtra was sorry for Draupadi's dishonour at the hands of Duryodhana. He set the Pandavas free and gave their kingdom back to them.

At this, Duryodhana was furious and said to his father, "Father, you have spoilt our victory. Now they will take revenge and kill us all. I will invite Yudhisthira again to a game of dice, and this time I will send them to exile. This time, the losing party will have to go for a twelve-year exile, followed by one year of hiding. If the winning party discovers them in hiding, the exile would have to be repeated." With the help of his wicked uncle, Shakuni, and his charmed dice, Duryodhana won the game and sent the Pandavas into twelve years of exile. He was sure that in the thirteenth year, he would discover them and send them back to another twelve years of exile.

Having lost the game of dice, the Pandavas went to live in the forests.

## 26 Sense of Responsibility

As Vikram lifted Betal again, Betal told Vikram another story. King Jayendra ruled his kingdom well. But his son Jai was irresponsible. Jayendra was worried that after his death Jai would not rule the kingdom well. He asked a sage to help him. The sage gave him a pot full of holy water. He said, "Take this to my ashram in the forest. Do not let even a drop spill because it will bring ill luck to your kingdom." Jai carefully took the pot and walked through the forest. He did not stop even to eat or drink and brought the pot to the ashram without spilling a drop. Next day, the king realised that Jai had become responsible. Betal asked Vikram, "What made Jai responsible?" Vikram said, "When he took care of the pot for one day he realised that taking care of the kingdom required the same responsibility." Hearing this Betal flew away.

## 27 The Magic Bowl

While the Pandavas were in exile, one day, the sun god gave Yudhisthira the bowl of plenty (*akshaypatra*) and said, "Give this to Draupadi. Once a day, she can take out as much food as she wants until she herself has eaten. Till then, this bowl will not run empty."

One day, Sage Durvasa and his disciples were passing through the forest. They came to the hut and asked Draupadi for some food. Draupadi had already eaten and she knew that the bowl wouldn't yield any more food.

Draupadi did not want to turn away the holy sages without food and prayed to Krishna, who came and said, "Give me some food." Draupadi said, "This is no time for jokes, please help me feed the guests." Krishna said, "That is why I ask for food." One grain of rice was left in the bowl, which she gave to Krishna. Krishna was satisfied, and surprisingly the guests too were satisfied. They left without asking for food.

## 28 Meenakshi

King Kulashekara of Manavur in South India was a devotee of Shiva. He even built a temple for Shiva. But, he was childless. Pleased with him, Parvati decided to take birth in his family. A daughter was born to Kulashekara with eyes like a fish. He named her Meenakshi, *meen* (meaning fish) and *askshi* (meaning eyes). She also smelled like a fish. When the baby was shown to a Brahmin, he said that her fish-like features would go away once she met her future husband. When she grew up, she went to Mount Kailash and saw Shiva. Immediately, her fish-like features disappeared. Meenakshi realised that Shiva was her future husband and they decided to get married. At their wedding, the gods came, but they refused to have food until Shiva danced his cosmic dance, the *chidambaram*.

# 29 The Sensitive Queens

Vikram went back to the tree and put Betal on his shoulders again. Betal started telling him another story.

King Jaipal had three queens. Each of them was very beautiful, sensitive, and fragile. One day, the first queen was wounded when a flower from her hair fell on her thigh. Another night when the king took the second queen to the terrace, the moonlight burned her skin. Another day when the third queen heard someone weeping in the next room, she became pale and fainted.

Betal asked Vikram, "Who was the most sensitive queen?" Vikram replied, "The third queen was the most sensitive because those who are sensitive to the suffering of others are truly sensitive." Betal was very happy with the answer. He said, "You are great, but you always make the mistake of breaking your silence. So I can't go with you." Saying this, Betal flew back to the tree.

# 30 Who Is the True Devotee

To prove the love of his devotees, one day, Krishna pretended that he had a headache. Krishna told Narada that he would recover only if a devotee smeared the dust from his feet on Krishna's forehead.

Startled at the remedy, Narada went to Krishna's queens for help. The queens shuddered at this proposal, because they felt that the gods would curse them for this disrespectful act. Then Narada went to the *gopis* and explained the purpose of his visit. He told them that Krishna's headache could be cured only with the dust from the feet of a true devotee. The *gopis* immediately collected some dust from their feet and gave it to Narada. Narada understood that the *gopis* loved Krishna blindly, so much that they could even risk not getting salvation to save him.

# 31 Narada and the Hunter

One day, while walking through the forests, Narada came across a deer lying on the ground. It had been pierced with an arrow and was writhing in pain. A little later, Narada saw a boar and then a rabbit, also injured and moaning in pain. Narada Muni was greatly pained at heart to see living beings suffer so. As he walked on, he came upon a hunter standing behind a tree. The hunter was lifting his bow to attack another animal.

Narada asked the hunter if he had injured the animals. The hunter nodded. Narada then asked him, "Why did you not kill the animals completely? Why did you half-kill them by piercing their bodies with arrows?"

The hunter replied that he drew pleasure from seeing the animals suffer to death. Narada was furious and told him that leaving harmless animals battered in this way meant giving them immense pain. He cursed the hunter, saying that if he did not stop doing so, the souls of the injured animals would return to haunt him.

The hunter grew worried and asked for forgiveness, but Narada said that he could be forgiven only if he performed severe penance.

Narada instructed the hunter to give up hunting and set up a small hut near the river. He told the hunter to plant a *tulsi* plant and worship it regularly.

After years, Narada found the hunter leading a pure life in the forests.

# Contents

*The Story of the Month:  How Garuda Became Vishnu's Mount*

The Story of the Month

# How Garuda Became Vishnu's Mount

## How Garuda Became Vishnu's Mount

Garuda wanted to get *amrit* from the gods to free himself and his mother, Vinata, from the slavery of his stepmother, Kadru, and his stepbrothers, the snakes. He asked his mother how he could get the *amrit*. Vinata replied, "You will have to fly to the kingdom of Indra, the king of the gods and get it. But for flying such a distance, you need to have lots of food to make you strong. You should go to the ocean and eat the Nishadas (a tribe of fishermen). This will satisfy your hunger. But a Brahmin lives with the Nishadas, do not eat him." Garuda followed his mother's instructions and ate the

Nishadas but by mistake he swallowed the Brahmin too. Soon after, he felt a fire burning in his throat and he immediately released the Brahmin. Even after eating the Nishadas, his hunger was not satisfied and so he went to his father, Sage Kashyapa.

Kashyapa said, "At some distance, you will find an elephant dragging a tortoise. The two of them were sages in their previous birth. They were brothers who had quarrelled over property. They had cursed each other to become an elephant and a tortoise. If you eat both of

them, your hunger will be satisfied." So Garuda went and ate the two animals. Then he flew towards the kingdom of Indra to get the *amrit*. When the gods came to know that Garuda was coming to take the *amrit* from them, a fierce battle started between them but Garuda defeated them easily. Then he went to the place where the *amrit* was kept. Huge flames surrounded the vessel containing the *amrit*. Garuda went to the ocean and swallowed lots of water to put out the flames. As he moved towards the *amrit*,

he noticed a big wheel with sharp spokes revolving in front of the vessel. Garuda became small in size and flew between the spokes of the wheel. Then he saw two ferocious animals guarding the vessel. He flapped his wings rapidly and blew dust into the eyes of the monsters and blinded them. Eventually, he reached the vessel and took it away using his talons.

Garuda could have drunk the *amrit* himself and become immortal but he had to offer it to the snakes to free his mother. This selfless act of Garuda impressed Vishnu, who granted him a

boon that he would become immortal even without drinking the *amrit*. But Vishnu asked him to prevent the snakes from drinking the *amrit*. Garuda took the *amrit* to the snakes who released Vinata and Garuda from slavery at once. As they were about to drink the *amrit*, Garuda stopped them and said that they should clean themselves first. The snakes agreed and went to clean themselves. In the meantime, the gods were furious with Garuda for stealing the *amrit* and wanted to stop him. Indra tried to attack Garuda and a battle followed.

Garuda smashed Indra's thunderbolt but Indra managed to escape with the *amrit*. However, a few drops of *amrit* fell on the ground and the snakes licked it. The *amrit* was so strong that it burnt their tongues and made them forked. This is the reason why snakes have forked tongues.

Meanwhile, Vishnu was watching everything from a distance and was pleased with Garuda's strength and determination. He made him the king of all birds. In return, Garuda agreed to become Vishnu's mount and since then, Vishnu is always accompanied by Garuda.

# 1 The Foolish Brothers

Vikram was once again carrying Betal on his shoulders while Betal narrated the story of the four foolish brothers.

Once, there were four brothers, who were very foolish. People used to make fun of them, and so one day, they decided to become learned. They went in four different directions with a promise that they would meet at the same place after ten years.

Ten years later when they met, they discussed with each other what they had learnt. The first brother said, "I can make a skeleton out of a single bone of an animal." The second said, "I can cover a skeleton with flesh." The third said, "I can cover a flesh-covered skeleton with skin and hair." The fourth said, " I can put life into a dead animal." They decided to demonstrate their skills. They found a bone and the first brother turned it into a skeleton, the second one covered it with flesh. The third one covered it with skin and hair. Now it looked like a dead lion. Then the fourth brother put life into the dead lion. As soon as the lion came to life, it killed all the four brothers and ate them up.

Betal paused and asked Vikram, "Who, according to you was responsible for the death of the four brothers?" Vikram replied, "The fourth brother was responsible for their deaths because he was foolish enough to put life in a dead lion. Without life, the lion could not have hurt them." Betal said, "O king, you are right, but you opened your mouth again, so here I go." Saying so, Betal flew back to the tree.

# 2 Arjuna's Search

When the Pandavas were in exile, Sage Vyasa told them, "After your exile, you will have a war with the Kauravas. Arjuna should pray to Shiva for divine weapons." Arjuna went to Mount Kailash and started worshipping Shiva. Pleased, Shiva disguised himself as a hunter and came to test Arjuna. Just then, a demon, Mooka, attacked Arjuna in the form of a wild boar. Arjuna shot an arrow and killed it. But he saw another arrow in the body of the boar. He said, "Who dare shoot my prey?" Shiva, in the hunter's form, said, "I shot the arrow. This is my prey." A long fight followed between the two and Arjuna became tired. He said, "I will fight after my prayers." Arjuna made a *Shivalinga* and put a garland around it. But to his dismay, he found the garland around the hunter's neck. He understood that the hunter was Shiva. Shiva came to his real form and gave him the *pashupatastra*.

# 3 Bhima and Kimira

Losing the game of dice to Duryodhana, the Pandavas were sent into exile for twelve years.

They were going through a forest where Kimira, a terrible demon, carrying a burning torch in his hand, stopped them. He roared and asked, "Who are you? This is my territory and you can't stay here." Yudhisthira introduced himself and his brothers. Enraged Kimira replied, "Bhima had killed my brother Bakasura and my friend Hidimb. He has disgraced us by marrying Hidimba, the demonness. Therefore I will kill him and take revenge." Saying this, he attacked Bhima who fought Kimira back. He uprooted a tree and hit Kimira with it. It was not long before Bhima strangled the demon to death.

# 4 Arjuna in Heaven

When Arjuna got the *pashupatastra* from Shiva, other gods also blessed him with more divine weapons. Varuna, the wind god gave him *varunapash*; Yama, the god of death gave him *dandastra*; Kubera gave him the *antardhyanastra*; and Indra gave the *vajrastra*. Indra also asked Arjuna to visit heaven and learn how to use the weapons. Indra's divine chariot, drawn by hundred horses, took him to heaven. There, a number of fairies and demi-gods welcomed him. The *gandharvas*, heavenly musicians, played melodious music for him. Arjuna stayed in Indra's palace and learnt how to use the weapons, after which he wanted to go back to earth. But Indra asked him to stay for some more time and learn to play the divine music of the *gandharvas*. Down on earth, the rest of the Pandavas were worried about the well-being of Arjuna. Soon Arjuna returned to them and showed all the weapons that he received.

## 5 Hanuman Meets Sita

When Hanuman reached Lanka, he saw Sita being tortured by the *rakshasis*. Hanuman thought it was important to assure Sita of her safety.

After the *rakshasis* had left, Hanuman came out of hiding.

Thinking that Sita might mistake him as Ravana's man, he narrated Rama's story and showed her his ring. Sita was overjoyed, but she also reminded Hanuman that only two months were left before Ravana would kill her.

At this Hanuman begged to take Sita across the ocean but Sita replied that Rama should himself come and take her back after defeating Ravana.

Hanuman promised her of their return. As he prepared to go, Sita handed over her jewellery to him as a token of her love for Rama.

## 6 The Greatest Sacrifice

As Vikram carried Betal, Betal started telling him another story.

Once Virsen, the king's guard, saw a woman crying. He asked her the reason, and she replied, "I am the goddess who protects the king. A demon has defeated me, so I will not be able to protect the king anymore. His life can be saved if you sacrifice your son to Kali." Virsen told this to his son who was ready to be sacrificed, so Virsen cut his head

in front of goddess Kali's idol. Virsen's wife was so heartbroken that she killed herself. Virsen was left all alone so he killed himself too. When the king heard about this, he felt guilty and killed himself.

Betal asked Vikram, "Whose sacrifice was the greatest?" Vikram replied, "The king's. The son died because it was his duty, Virsen and his wife died because they lost their son, the king however had no reason to die." Betal heard this and flew away.

# 7 The Syamantaka Jewel

Once there lived a king by the name of Satrajit. He had secured the precious jewel, Syamantaka, from Surya. Satrajit was very fond of the jewel and always kept it with himself. One day, Krishna arrived in his court and asked for the jewel, but Satrajit refused to give it to him.

One day, when Satrajit was out of the palace, his younger brother Prasena stole the jewel from the safe and wore it during a hunting expedition. Unfortunately, the jewel fell on the ground when Prasena died fighting a lion. Jambavan, Sugreeva's minister, found the jewel and gave it to his son to play.

Satrajit discovered that the jewel was no longer in the safe. When Prasena did not return he thought Krishna had forcefully taken the jewel after killing him. When Krishna heard this, he immediately set out to look for the jewel. On reaching the forest, he found Jambavan's son playing with it.

Thinking Krishna to be a thief, Jambavan attacked him, but he soon recognised him and begged forgiveness. He returned the jewel to Krishna and also asked him to marry his daughter Jambavati.

Accompanied by his newly wedded wife, Jambavati, Krishna returned victorious to his palace in Dwarka. One day, he visited Satrajit's court and returned the jewel in front of everyone.

Satrajit felt ashamed for foolishly accusing Krishna and asked for mercy. He asked Krishna to marry his daughter Satyabhama. Krishna married her in a grand ceremony. When it was time for Krishna to leave, Satrajit also offered him the Syamantaka, but Krishna refused to accept it.

# 8 Hanuman Destroys Vatika

As Hanuman was preparing to leave Lanka, he decided to do something to show his strength to the enemy. He started destroying Vatika. In the process, all the birds flew out of the trees, and the noise awakened the *rakshasis*. Hanuman decided to wait at the gate to see the consequences.

As the news of this destruction reached Ravana, he sent Kikkar, Durjaya, and Jaambmalee, his most ferocious demons, to fight Hanuman. Hanuman killed them one after another. Ravana then sent his ministers to arrest the powerful monkey. Hanuman destroyed the ministers and their powerful armies in a matter of minutes. Finally, realising that Hanuman was a divine soul, Ravana decided to send his own son Akshaya.

As the powerful Akshaya approached, Hanuman grabbed him and flung him in the air. The death of Akshaya scared Ravana. He now decided to send Meghnad to kill Hanuman.

## 9 Andal's Devotion

Like Krishna's *gopis*, Andal had conquered Vishnu by her love and devotion. Her father was Periaazhvaar, a Vishnu devotee, who found her abandoned at the Srivilliputtur Vishnu temple when she was young. As she grew older, her love for Vishnu deepened. One day, Periaazhvaar found her wearing the garlands of the temple's deity. When he asked her, she said, "I am wearing the god's garlands whom I shall marry." Angry, Periaazhvaar made fresh garlands. That night Vishnu appeared in his dream and said that he would only accept the garlands that Andal had worn. Now Andal understood her divine nature and offered her at the Ranganatha temple at Srirangam. Ranganatha is another name of Vishnu. While she was being offered, Andal disappeared and merged herself with the idol. Andal is also known as Goda, or Bhuma devi.

## 10 Bhima Meets Hanuman

One day, while the Pandavas were in exile, the wind brought a beautiful lotus and dropped it near Draupadi. She was delighted with its sweet fragrance and divine beauty. She asked Bhima to bring her more lotuses.

Bhima went in search of lotuses. As he was walking through the forest, he saw an old monkey sleeping in his path. He made a sound to scare it away. But it did not move. Bhima ordered the monkey to give him way. The monkey said, "I am too old and weak to move. Push my tail aside to make way for yourself." Bhima tried very hard to move its tail but failed. He understood that the monkey was some great being. The monkey come to his real form. He was Hanuman. Hanuman blessed Bhima and promised to help him in the war against Kauravas.

## 11 Ekadanta

Once, Parashurama visited Mount Kailash, the home of Shiva. As Shiva was asleep, Ganesha stopped Parashurama from awakening his father. Parashurama threw his axe angrily, which he had got from Shiva, at Ganesha. Ganesha recognised his father's axe and received it with respect. The axe cut one of his tusks. Since then Ganesha is called Ekadanta, which means one-toothed.

# 12 Hanuman Meets Meghnad

Meghnad, Ravana's son, had mastered the art of warfare from Brahma. Hearing about the destruction that Hanuman inflicted, Meghnad took his father's blessing and set out to kill him.

Hanuman crushed all the arrows that Meghnad shot. Finally, Meghnad decided to use *brahmaastra*. It had the power to tie even Hanuman. As Meghnad shot the arrow, it wound around Hanuman. However, Hanuman was not scared, as Brahma had given him a boon that the *brahmaastra* could tie him only for some time. The *rakshasis* came charging at him without knowing that the *brahmaastra* would lose its power on being touched. So, just as the *rakshasis* touched him, Hanuman started reviving. Meghnad, who knew that *every minute* was precious, quickly tied Hanuman and dragged him to Ravana's court.

# 13 Meerabai's Devotion

Meerabai was born to the Rajput king, Rana Ratan Singh, in Rajasthan. From a very young age she became a devotee of Krishna and wrote poems in his praise. As she grew older, her love and devotion for Krishna increased.

Meerabai was married at a tender age and lost her husband very soon. At her in-laws' house, she devoted herself entirely to Krishna.

Her in-laws did not understand her devotion and objected to this outward display of affection for another man and attempted to kill her. They tortured her and tried to cause her harm. Even when being tortured by her in-laws, Meerabai only chanted the name of Krishna.

She finally escaped and settled down in Dwarka. There, she dedicated her life entirely to singing and composing poems about her God.

# 14 Kumudini

Vikram picked up Betal on his shoulders again. Betal narrated the story of Kumudini, the orphan girl, to Vikram. Kumudini lived with her relatives who made her work all day. No one loved her and so she wept all night. Her weeping disturbed her neighbour Kundan. Kundan went to a sage and told him about Kumudini. The sage asked Kundan to bring her to his ashram. Kumudini started living in the ashram and she was happy. After some years,

Kundan was passing through the forest and saw Kumudini, who had grown very beautiful. Kundan asked her to marry him, but she refused. Kundan thought that Kumudini was ungrateful; it was he who had brought her to the ashram where she could live happily. Betal asked Vikram, "Was she ungrateful?" Vikram replied, "No, Kundan had taken the girl to the ashram because he didn't want to be disturbed by her weeping, he didn't do it out of concern for her." Betal heard this and flew away.

# 15 Hanuman Meets Ravana

When Hanuman entered Ravana's courtroom, he saw him sitting on a diamond-studded throne. Shining bright in his royal dress, Ravana was surrounded by beautiful angels.

Ravana asked Hanuman the purpose of his visit.

Hanuman proudly replied that he was Rama's messenger and had come to free Sita from his cluthes. He also tried to explain that whatever Ravana was doing was unlawful. Hearing Hanuman speak this way, Ravana was very angry. He immediately asked his men to kill the impolite monkey,

but just then, Vibhishana, Ravana's younger brother, intervened.

Vibhishana, who was tired of Ravana's misdeeds, tried to explain that killing an envoy in this manner was not right, and a less severe punishment should be given. Ravana was furious with his brother.

## 16 Parashurama

Sage Jamadagni was once performing a *yajna* in his ashram. He asked his wife, Renuka, to get water from the river Ganga. Renuka went to the river where she found some *gandharvas* (heavenly beings) enjoying themselves. She stood looking at them and got late. Jamadagni was very angry. He ordered his sons to kill their mother, Renuka. His sons were shocked. They stood silent. This further enraged Jamadagni. Just then,

Parashurama, another son of Jamadagni entered with Renuka. Jamadagni ordered him to kill his mother and his brothers. Without hesitating, Parashurama raised his axe and chopped their heads off. By now, Jamadagni's anger had cooled down. He was pleased with Parashurama's devotion and gave him a wish. Parashurama asked him to bring his mother and brothers back to life. Jamadagni granted his wish. This is how he saved his mother and brothers from the wrath of his father.

## 17 Krishna Kills Satadhanva

Krishna refused to accept the Syamantaka jewel from Satrajit, and told him to keep it safely, as it had the power to wipe out all sorrow, and destruction. The news of the jewel spread like wild fire. A lot of people desired to own the jewel. A wicked man, Satadhanva, led one such group. One day, he broke into Satrajit's chamber to steal the Syamantaka. When the king protested, Satadhanva killed him mercilessly.

Satrajit's daughter, Satyabhama quickly informed Krishna about the gruesome incident. Upon hearing the news, Krishna lamented the loss of the noble king and vowed to recover the jewel at any cost. Krishna, accompanied by Balarama, arrived at Dwarka to search for Satadhanva. Meanwhile, Satadhanva, upon

hearing Krishna's arrival, fled the city of Dwarka to seek refuge at his friend Akrura's house.

Akrura refused help saying that they could not fight Krishna. Just as Satadhanva left Akrura's house Krishna arrived. He caught hold of Satadhanva and killed him. However, Krishna knew that

Satadhnava was not alone in the conspiracy. He called a meeting at his court and asked Akrura to show the jewel. Everybody was startled to hear Akrura's name. Krishna, being the Almighty, knew that his uncle too was part of this wrong deed. Akrura fell at Krishna's feet, and asked for forgiveness.

# 18 Bhima and the Python

One day while the Pandavas were in exile, Bhima went in search of food for all of them. Looking around in the forest, he saw a cave and entered it.

A massive python was sitting near the entrance of the cave. When it saw Bhima, it attacked him and coiled itself round his body. Bhima was helpless and struggled hard to free himself from the python's grip but his attempts to save himself seemed ineffective. Finally, he got tired and gave up. Then he asked the python, "Who are you and why have you entangled me like this for no reason? I have not caused you any harm." The python replied, "I am your ancestor. In my previous birth I had insulted a sage and was cursed to become a python. Now, I will eat you if you don't answer my questions correctly."

Meanwhile, back at their hut, the rest of the Pandavas began to worry since Bhima had not returned and it was getting dark. Since Bhima was very strong and powerful, they had never imagined that any harm could come to him.

Anxious, they went out to search for him. On the way, they saw many dead animals and their anxiety grew. Finally, when they reached the mouth of the cave, they saw Bhima struggling to free himself from the python's grip.

Yudhisthira, who was known to be very wise answered all the questions of the python correctly and freed Bhima from his clutches. Not only this, the python was also freed from his curse and he thanked the Pandavas and ascended to heaven. The Pandavas returned home safely.

# 19 Krishna and Kalindi

One day Krishna and Arjuna went out on a hunting expedition.

As the day drew to a close, they decided to bathe in the waters of the Yamuna. Just then, Krishna spotted a beautiful maiden passing by the river. Krishna immediately sent Arjuna after her.

When asked to reveal her identity, she replied, "I'm Kalindi, the daughter of the sun god. I worship Krishna and hope to marry him one day."

Arjuna then asked her why she was staying alone. Kalindi promptly answered, "So that nobody disturbs me during my prayers." She continued, "I hope that one day my wish will come true and the Krishna will take me under his protection."

Seeing the staunch devotion of Kalindi, Arjuna was pleased and went back to Krishna to tell him about her love for him and her wish. Touched by Kalindi's pure love, Krishna decided to marry her and make her his queen.

## 20 The Supreme Sacrifice

Once, Vritrasur, a powerful demon, wanted to conquer heaven. He fought with the gods and swallowed all their weapons. The gods went to Vishnu. Vishnu said, "Due to long penance, the bones of Dhadichi, the sage, have become very strong. Only the weapon made of his bones can kill Vritrasur. But you can't kill Dhadichi, as he is my devotee. You will have to ask him to die to give his bones." The gods, led by Indra, went to Dhadichi and begged for his bones. Dhadichi was ready to sacrifice his life, but he wanted to go on a pilgrimage before that. Hearing this, Indra brought all the holy places near him. After taking dips in the holy waters, Dhadichi gave up his life. Indra made a weapon called *Vajra* with his bones and killed Vritrasur.

## 21 Hanuman Sets Lanka on Fire

Ravana was furious that Hanuman had come to Lanka as Rama's messenger. He ordered Vibhishana to set Hanuman's tail on fire and take him in a procession through the streets of Lanka.

Accordingly, Hanuman's tail was tied with a rope and set on fire. As Hanuman walked down the streets, people laughed at him.

Sita begged Agnideva not to hurt Hanuman. Agnideva cooled his flames and though Hanuman's tail was still ablaze, it did not hurt him. Meanwhile, Hanuman decided to have some fun. Shrinking in size he quickly shook off the rope. Then leaping from building to building, he set them on fire. Soon the entire city of Lanka was burning.

Fearing that his prank might have hurt Sita, Hanuman rushed to see her but was relieved to see her safe.

Then bidding her farewell, he jumped into the sea and swam across to Rama.

## 22 Duryodhana Visits the Pandavas

The Pandavas were facing many hardships during their exile. A Brahmin visited Dhritarashtra and told him about their hard life. Dritarashtra felt sorry but Karna said, "It would be great if we could see the condition of the Pandavas." Duryodhana agreed and, accompanied by Shakuni, they went to where the Pandavas were staying. They put up their tents near the Pandavas' hut and made fun of them. One day Duryodhana and his companions went to a lake for bathing. At that time, Chitrasen, the king of the *gandharvas* (heavenly beings) also came to the lake. There was a fight between Duryodhana's party and the *gandharvas*. Scared, Karna fled. Chitrasen used his Sammohanastra to make Duryodhana motionless and captured him.

## 23 The Prophecy

As Vikram lifted Betal on his shoulders once again, Betal told Vikram another story

Once, there lived a woodcutter who was very hardworking but poor. He asked a sage, "Will I ever become rich?" The sage read his palm and said, "No matter how you hard you work, you will never become rich. If you become rich, you will die." The woodcutter was disheartened, but he continued to work hard. One day, he found a pot of gold in the forest. He remembered the sage's prophecy but thought, "One day everyone has to die, and it is no use leaving this pot here." He took the gold with him and used it to help the villagers. He did not die early and lived a long life. Betal asked Vikram, "Was the sage's prophecy wrong?" Vikram replied, "No. Since the woodcutter did not spend the gold on himself, he was not actually rich and therefore he did not die." Betal said, "Very good, but I have to go."

# 24 Krishna and Bhaumasura

Bhaumasura was a powerful demon. He was very fond of young girls and travelled from one kingdom to the other kidnapping young maidens. In this way he had captured sixteen thousand one hundred women and made them his slaves. The girls prayed to Indra for help. Indra went to Krishna and asked him to free the girls from Bhaumasura.

Vishnu's mount Garuda transported Krishna to Bhaumasura's capital city, Pragjyotisapura. There, Krishna found that the city was heavily fortified with gigantic walls, barbed wire, weapons, and soldiers.

Fearless Krishna sounded his arrival by blowing his conch shell. He fired his *Sudarshan Chakra* at the walls and his arrows at the soldiers. When Maura, the demon who had built the city, came to see the damage caused by Krishna, he too was killed. The news of Krishna's arrival spread like wildfire. Next, Maura's seven sons came charging, but Krishna defeated them all.

Finally, Bhaumasura himself came forward. He fired the *sataghni*, which could demolish a huge army at once. Krishna retaliated with his feathered arrow and stopped the *sataghni* midway. Meanwhile, Garuda too had launched his attack. Bhaumasura shot a series of arrows at the bird, but they broke as soon as they hit his strong body.

Frustrated, Bhaumasura finally decided to attack with the trident, but before he could even lay his hands on it, Krishna cut off his head with the *Sudarshan Chakra*. The girls fell in love with their saviour and wished to marry him. Krishna returned with them to Dwarka and fulfilled their wishes.

# 25 The Sacrifice

As Vikram carried Betal, he narrated another story. One day, a king went hunting in the forest and lost his way. A man named Rajdeep helped. The king made him his guard. One day, Rajdeep met a beautiful girl Deepti and asked her to marry him. Deepti agreed and Rajdeep took her to the king. On meeting the king Deepti asked him to marry her. On hearing this, Rajdeep was hurt, but he agreed. The king asked her, "Why do you want to marry me instead of Rajdeep?" Deepti replied, "Because I want to live in a palace." The king gave Rajdeep a palace and asked Deepti to marry him. Betal asked Vikram, "Whose sacrifice was greater, the king's or Rajdeep's?"

Vikram replied, "The king's, because Rajdeep was only being loyal to his master and even if he wanted he couldn't stop Deepti from marrying the king." Betal heard this and flew away.

## 26 Krishna Marries Five Queens

When Mitravinda, princess of the kingdom of Avanti, chose Krishna over Duryodhana at her *swayamvara*, he was furious. He watched helplessly as Krishna took his bride away with him.

The religious king of Kausalya, Nagnajit, had a very beautiful daughter named Satya, also called Nagnajiti. Nagnajit had laid down the condition that only a brave man who could tame seven wild bulls could marry Satya. When Krishna arrived, Nagnajit was overwhelmed to see a god and he secretly wished Krishna to marry his daughter. Krishna won the challenge and married Satya.

Next, the kings of the Kaikeya kingdom offered their sister, Bhadra, to the god in a grand ceremony. When Laksmana, daughter of the king of Madra prayed to Krishna, he appeared at her *swayamvara* and married her.

## 27 Hanuman Returns to Rama

Hanuman returned from Lanka after meeting Sita and setting Lanka on fire. Sugreeva congratulated Hanuman on his brave deed and honoured him at a ceremony.

When Rama saw them rejoicing, he grew restless and enquired about Sita and her well-being.

Hanuman turned to Rama and gave a detailed report of his stay in Lanka. When he narrated the stories about Sita's torture, tears welled up in Rama's eyes. Hanuman also told Rama that only a few months were left before Ravana would kill Sita if she did not agree to marry him.

After handing over the piece of jewellery Sita had given, Hanuman said, "O lord, Sita loves you dearly. She is eagerly waiting for you to rescue her."

Embracing Hanuman, Rama thanked him for his selfless service.

## 28 Preparation for War

When Hanuman described Ravana's strengths and weaknesses, everyone started preparing for the war. Weapons were collected and divisions in the army were formed. Rama chose experienced warriors like Gaj, Gavay, and Gavaaksh to lead the guard. While preparing for the battle, Rama saw some good omens and understood that he would be victorious.

# 29 Pandavas Save Duryodhana

Duryodhana had come to the forest where the Pandavas were spending their years in exile. There, Chitrasena, the king of the Gandharvas imprisoned him. On hearing this, Yudhisthira said to Arjuna, "We can settle scores with Duryodhana later. An outsider has captured our cousin. It is a question of honour of our clan, so go and rescue Duryodhana." Arjuna went and defeated Chitrasena's soldiers. Chitrasena was forced to descend from heaven. He was Arjuna's friend. He told Arjuna, "Indra had ordered me to punish Duryodhana and his friends for making fun of you." Arjuna took Chitrasena to Yudhisthira who said, "We thank you for your concern for us. But please release Duryodhana now." Chitrasena agreed and released Duryodhana. Duryodhana felt very humiliated because his most hated enemies, the Pandavas, saved his life.

# 30 Indrajit and Vibhishana

Ravana called his council of ministers to discuss how to fight with Rama.

At this meeting, Vibhishana was also present. He warned Ravana, "Brother, please give up your desire of marrying Sita. Rama is a mighty warrior. Your sinful actions will bring disaster."

Hearing Vibhishana speak his way, Indrajit replied, "You are a coward and a traitor. Instead of supporting us you're speaking on behalf of Rama."

Vibhishana tried to explain that a hasty decision could destroy everyone but voices of protest arose as he spoke. Everybody urged Ravana to fight the monkey brigade led by Rama.

Encouraged by his ministers, Ravana said to Vibhishana, "You have spoken in favour of my enemy. You are a shame to our race. Go away before I kill you."

# Contents

*The Story of the Month:   Wise Yudhisthira*

The Story of the Month

# Wise Yudhisthira

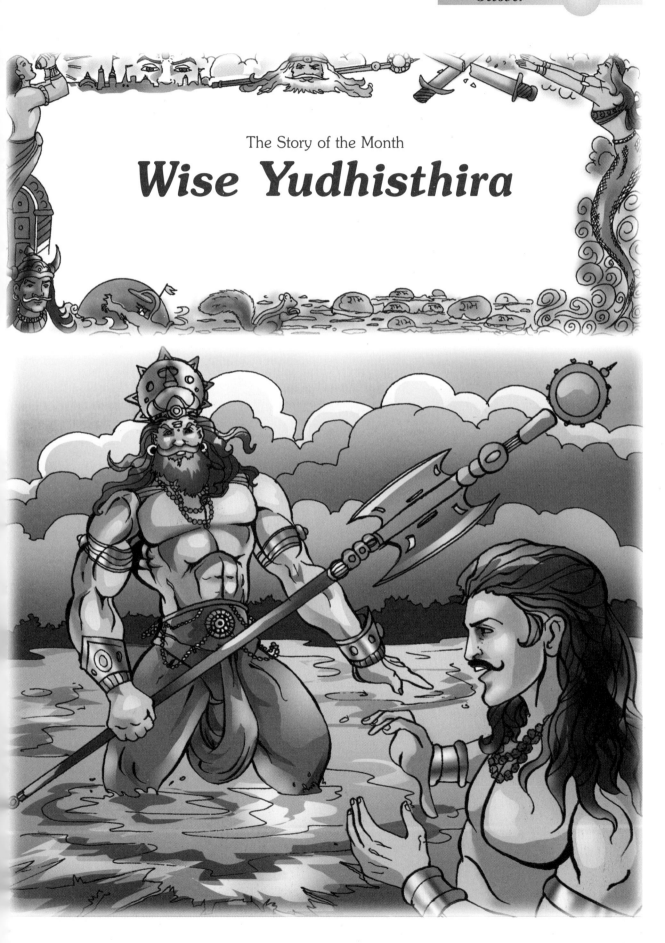

# Wise Yudhisthira

Once, a strange incident occurred with the Pandavas while they were in the forest during their years in exile.

One day, a Brahmin came to them and said, "I hang the sticks by which I produce fire for my *yajnas* on a tree. This morning a stag came and rubbed its horns against the tree. My sticks fell and got stuck in the stag's horns and the stag ran away with them. I want you to get my sticks back."

The Pandavas agreed and went in search of the stag. They found it but before they could shoot, it ran away. By now the Pandavas were thirsty and tired. They decided to rest in the shade of a tree. Yudhisthira asked Nakula to climb a tree and see if there was water around. Nakula climbed a tree and saw a pool of water. Yudhisthira asked him to bring water for all of them. Nakula went to the pool, but as he tried to take some water in his hands, he heard a voice, "This pool belongs to me. Before taking water from here, you will have to answer my questions." Nakula was very thirsty and ignored the warning. But as soon as he touched the water he fainted.

After sometime, Yudhisthira sent Sahadeva to look for him. Sahadeva came to the pool and found Nakula unconscious. He decided to sprinkle some water on Nakula's face to awaken him. But as Sahadeva tried to take water from the pool, he heard the same warning. He too ignored the warning and became unconscious. Then Arjuna came in search of his brothers. He reached the pool and was very angry to see the state of his brothers. He roared, "Who dared to hurt my brothers. Come before me and I will teach you a lesson." But there was no reply. So he decided to take some water from the pool to awaken his brothers. But the moment he tried to touch the water, he heard the voice,

"You can't take water before answering my questions. Your brothers ignored my warning and that is why they are lying unconscious." Arjuna's anger knew no bounds. He said, "No one can stop me from taking the water." As he touched the water he too fainted.

When Arjuna did not return Yudhisthira sent Bhima, who met with the same fate. Yudhisthira was getting worried; none of his four brothers had returned. This time, he himself went to look for them and came to the pool. He was very sad to see his brothers lying unconscious. He also

tried to take some water from the pool and heard the same voice: "You can't take water from here before answering my questions. The other four men ignored my warning and look at them now." Yudhisthira said, "You seem to be a divine being. Please ask me the questions. I will try to answer them."

Now Yudhisthira was famous for his wisdom. He was also called Dharmaraja for his knowledge of religion. The strange voice asked him many questions about religion and Yudhisthira replied carefully and correctly.

In the end, the voice said, "Since I am very pleased with your wisdom. I will bring one of your brothers to their senses. You can choose one of your brothers." Yudhisthira said, "We five brothers are sons of two mothers, Kunti and Madri. I am Kunti's son so please bring one of Madri's sons back to his senses." Hearing this reply the voice said, "You have again pleased me with your impartial judgement." Suddenly, Yama, the god of death, appeared. The voice was of Yama. He brought all the four Pandavas back to their senses.

# 1 The Girl in the Dream

Betal once again narrated a story to Vikram.

Manikdweep was ruled by a king named Mani Verma. His son, Sudhir, was very dutiful. When Sudhir reached twenty, Mani Verma decided to get him married to a beautiful girl. Finally, the king selected the princess of a neighbouring kingdom.

That night he saw a beautiful dream—a fair, doe-eyed girl with her arms open, waiting to embrace him. Sudhir woke up startled. Completely smitten by this dream he decided to delay his marriage and hunt for the girl. Taking permission from his father he left the palace dressed as a commoner.

He searched villages, towns, and cities. For three months he travelled thus but the girl was nowhere to be found. Tired, he decided to take a break near a river. There he spotted a girl with her back turned to him. Curious, he went up to her.

Just as she turned his heart skipped a beat—before him stood his dream girl. Excited, he proposed marriage to her. On hearing a stranger speak this way the girl complained to her father. When Sudhir came to meet him, he asked, "Who are you and why are you chasing my daughter?"

Sudhir felt ashamed and kept mum. He returned home and married the princess.

Betal asked Vikram, "Why did Sudhir feel ashamed?" "He realised he was foolishly running after a dream about which he knew nothing," Vikram replied.

"Right again," cried Betal and flew away.

# 2 Krishna and Banasura

Banasura was a demon who worshipped Shiva. Pleased with his devotion, Shiva promised to fulfil his wish. The arrogant Bana asked Shiva to guard his gates. Shiva took great offence at this but had to agree because he had already given his word. Eventually, Bana became more powerful and one day he expressed his wish to fight with someone. Shiva said his wish would be fulfilled when the flagstaff on his palace was broken.

Bana's daughter, Usha, loved Krishna's grandson Aniruddha. Bana did not like this. Once, when Aniruddha came, Bana captured him. Narada informed Krishna about the incident. Krishna arrived at Bana's palace and broke his flagstaff. Recognising the signal, Bana attacked him. Krishna won the battle and was about to kill Bana when Shiva begged him to spare Bana's life. Krishna agreed on the condition that Bana apologised for his mistakes. Bana then asked Shiva to forgive him.

# 3 Yudhisthira Gets Boons

Yudhisthira had answered all the questions of Yama and saved his brothers. Yama was very happy with him and promised him two boons. Yudhisthira said, "We had come here to get the igniting sticks of a Brahmin that were stuck in a stag's horn. As my first wish please help me get those sticks." Yama replied, "That stag was no one but me in disguise. This whole incident was just to test you." Saying so, Yama returned the two sticks. Then Yudhisthira said, "We have to spend the thirteenth year of our exile in hiding. As my second boon, please grant us that we are not found out while we are in hiding." Yama granted him the boon and instructed, "All of you should go to Viratnagar. Nobody will be able to trace you there."

# 4 King Nriga and Krishna

Nriga was a good and kind king. He regularly gave gifts and alms to the needy and the poor.

One day, he promised to give a flock of cows to a Brahmin. After some time, when a beggar arrived at his gates, Nriga gave the cows to him. The Brahmin became furious at being ignored this way. He cursed Nriga to turn into a chameleon and live in a dry well, located near Dwarka, forever.

One day, some children from Krishna's family came to play near this well. While playing, their ball fell into the well. When the boys came to search for the ball, they were surprised to see the huge chameleon. Scared at the sight, they rushed to Krishna for help.

Krishna lowered his hands to fetch him out. As soon as he touched it, the chameleon changed into Nriga.

Nriga narrated his story and then thanked Krishna for his divine touch that gave back his life.

## 5 The Parijataka Tree

During *samudra manthan* (churning of the ocean), the gods had obtained Parijataka, the tree with divine fragrance. This tree was planted in the garden of Indra, the king of gods. One day, Sage Narada went to this garden and collected some flowers that had fallen from the tree and gave them to Rukmini, Krishna's wife. Rukmini was very happy but when Satyabhama, another wife of Krishna, smelled its fragrance, she asked Krishna to bring her the tree. After defeating Indra, Krishna brought the tree on earth. But, a quarrel started between Rukmini and Satyabhama, as both of them wanted the tree. Krishna planted the tree in Satyabhama's courtyard in such a way that its flowers fell in Rukmini's house and in this way both his wives were happy.

## 6 The Generous King

Betal told another story.

A benevolent king used to give huge amounts of money in charity. His minister Surya Prakash understood the value of money and advised the king to donate wisely.

One day, when Surya Prakash went to the river he saw a beautiful maiden perched on a floating branch of a tree. He swam across to meet her.

She said she was a *nag* princess and that a wicked demon had captured her kingdom. He would set it free only if he was given another empire in return. The minister rushed back to inform the king about her.

Pained by her tale, the king gave away his own kingdom and went underwater with her. Surya Prakash blamed himself for the king's disappearance and killed himself.

Now Betal asked, "Who was really responsible?" Vikram replied, "Surya Prakash, because as the king's minister he was aware of his master's overly generous nature, yet he told him of the princess's problem."

# 7 Jaidratha's Punishment

The Pandavas faced many problems during their exile. One day, the Pandavas had gone to look for food and Draupadi was alone in their hut. Jaidratha, the king of Sindhudesha passed by the hut and saw Draupadi. Jaidratha was fascinated by Draupadi's beauty. He approached her and introduced himself. Draupadi remembered that the king of Sindhudesha was the husband of Dushshala, Duryodhana's sister. So she invited Jaidratha into the hut because he was a relative of the Pandavas. Jaidratha said, "You are so beautiful. Why are you undergoing the hardships of exile with the Pandavas? Come with me, I will make you my queen." Draupadi felt very insulted when she heard this. She said, "How dare you say that to me. The Pandavas will kill you." Jaidratha said, "I am

not afraid of them. They are no more than beggars now." He forced Draupadi into his chariot and took her away.

Soon the Pandavas returned to their hut and found Draupadi missing. They were told everything. Bhima was very angry; once again the honour of the Pandavas was at stake. He took his chariot and followed Jaidratha. He captured Jaidratha and dragged him by his hair to Yudhisthira.

Draupadi was crying bitterly. Seeing this, Bhima asked his elder brother's permission to kill Jaidratha. Yudhisthira said, "Jaidratha is our sister's husband. If we kill him, our sister would be widowed. Let us punish him suitably but spare his life." Draupadi said, "By insulting me, he has dishonoured you all. Shave his head but leave five tufts of hair on it. This will be a fitting insult for dishonouring the Pandavas."

# 8 Paundraka Challenges Krishna

Paundraka was the king of the Karusa province. He was very vain and thought himself to be the most powerful man in the universe.

One day, the king sent his messenger to Krishna. The messenger read out , "Krishna, give up your false pretence of being a god because I'm the supreme power. Come and surrender to me or else I shall kill you."

Everyone was startled to hear this. Krishna patiently lis-

tened and then replied, "Tell your master that I called him a foolish person. He has unknowingly challenged me. I shall destroy him."

Being threatened this way Paundraka, together with his friend, the king of Kasi, attacked Krishna. At the battlefield Krishna said, "You had asked me to give my divine symbols to you. So here it is." Saying this, Krishna flung his divine weapon, the *Sudarshan Chakra,* at Paundraka and cut off his head and killed him.

## 9 Vibhisana Meets Rama

Ravana expelled his younger brother Vibhisana from Lanka because he tried to discourage Ravana from fighting with Rama. Vibhisana decided to go to Rama and help him.

Seeing Vibhisana, Sugreeva and the others grew suspicious, but Hanuman assured them of his honest nature. Like a loyal servant, Vibhisana told Rama about Ravana's strengths and weaknesses. He explained that Ravana had been granted the boon of immortality by Brahma. He gave Rama all the details of Ravana's weapons, soldiers, army, and methods of warfare. He also told them about Indrajit's ability to disappear while fighting the enemy.

All this valuable information helped Rama decide how to organise his army and fight Ravana. Finally, Vibhisana suggested that Rama should pray to Samudra to help him build the bridge to Lanka and cross the sea.

Rama warmly hugged Vibhisana and thanked him for all his help. Rama promised to crown Vibhisana the king of Lanka after defeating Ravana and freeing Sita from his clutches.

## 10 Jaidratha's Boons

Jaidratha was humiliated by the way the Pandavas punished him. He could not go back to his kingdom with his head shaven, so he stayed back in the forest. He performed *tapasya*. Pleased with his devotion, Shiva appeared and granted him a boon. Jaidratha asked that he could defeat the Pandavas. Shiva said, "It is not possible. But in a battle you will be able to stop all the Pandavas, except Arjuna, for a day.

## 11 Rama and the Squirrel

Rama wanted to cross the bridge to Lanka in order to save Sita from Ravana's clutches. He sat down to pray to the sea god. The sea god, Samudra, arose from the depths of the sea and told Rama to build a bridge across the sea.

All the monkeys got busy building the bridge by placing boulders. A tiny squirrel was watching everything from his burrow. He decided to help Rama. He began picking sand and scattered twigs and scurried back and forth from the shore to the sea. Little by little the squirrel had gathered an entire heap.

Rama noticed the dedication of this tiny creature. Picking it up on his palm, he warmly stroked the animal with his three fingers. Since then, it is believed that squirrels have three lines on their body.

## 12 Pandavas in Hiding

During their thirteenth year of exile, the Pandavas decided to stay in Viratnagar in the disguise of Brahmins. There they got jobs in King Virata's palace.

Yudhisthira became the king's advisor under the name of Kanka. Bhima became the royal cook under the name of Vallabha. Draupadi became the maid of the queen under the name of Sairandhri. But she put three conditions for her service—she would not clean dirty utensils, she would not eat leftover food, and she would not wash anybody's feet.

Arjuna, who had learnt music, became the royal musician under the name of Brihnnala.

Nakula and Sahadeva also got suitable jobs. Meanwhile, in Hastinapur, Duryodhana was thinking of evil plans to find the Pandavas and send them to another twelve years of exile and so he sent his spies all around the country to look for them.

## 13 Krishna and Sudaksina

When Kasi was killed by Krishna, his son Sudaksina vowed to take revenge.

He prayed to Shiva to help him. Pleased with his devotion, Shiva advised him to perform black magic and acquire an evil spirit to kill his enemy.

Accordingly, Sudaksina performed a demonic sacrifice. After a while, Daksinagni, the demon, emerged from the blazing fire. It had long sharp teeth, a huge red tongue, and a blazing trident.

Following Sudaksina's instructions, the demon went to Dwarka. As he placed his huge steps, the city trembled and all the people fled. The guards rushed to inform Krishna about the appearance of this fearsome demon. Recognising Daksinagni, Krishna flung the *Sudarshan Chakra* at him. Seeing the *chakra,* the demon fled. If the effects of black magic fail, the demon returns to kill its creator. Accordingly, Daksinagni went to kill Sudaksina while the *chakra* followed. After his death, the *chakra* returned to Dwarka.

## 14 Bhima and Kichaka

Draupadi was living in Viratnagar as the queen's maid. Kichaka was the queen's brother and the general of the Viratnagar army. King Virata was weak, so all the powers were in the hands of Kichaka. One day, Kichaka saw Draupadi and fell in love with her. Considering her one of the queen's maids, he offered to marry her. Draupadi warned him not to trouble her. Kichaka got angry at the boldness of a maid and dragged her to the king's court. He kicked and insulted her. Crying bitterly, Draupadi came to Bhima, who was working as the royal cook and asked him to kill Kichaka. Bhima was very angry and killed Kichaka. The news of the death of Kichaka, who was a great warrior, spread like fire, and eventually Duryodhana came to know about it and realised that the Pandavas were in Viratnagar.

# 15 Dvivida and Balarama

Dvivida, the gorilla, was a dear friend of Bhaumasura who had been killed by Krishna. To avenge the death of his friend, he decided to destroy Dwarka.

He kidnapped young girls, killed sages, and set fire to villages. One day while uprooting a mountain, the melodious sounds of the flute reached his ears. Following the sound, he went to a cave and discovered Balarama playing the flute for the *gopis*.

Dvivida decided to create some mischief there. He created all sorts of noise, made faces at Balarama, and broke tree branches. Balarama decided to teach him a lesson.

He took his club and attacked Dvivida. The gorilla pulled out a huge oak tree and went charging at Balarama. Balarama crushed the tree with his feet.

Balarama then launched a blow on his face. Dvivida's jaw shook and all his teeth fell out. Then with another punch of his powerful fist Balram killed the animal.

# 16 Rama Crosses the Sea

To cross the sea and go to Lanka, Rama shot his arrows through the water. The sea god, Samudra appeared before Rama. With hands folded he said that if the sea dried, the natural balance would be affected. He suggested that Rama should consult Nal, Vishwakarma's able son and a soldier in Sugreeva's army, to construct a bridge. Accordingly Nal laid out a plan for the construction. All the monkeys got together to build the bridge. Large trees, bamboos, huge rocks, and a lot of sand were used to construct the platform.

When Nal finished building the bridge , all the gods including Samudra came to see it. They admired his work and showered petals on it. Once it was constructed, Samudra assured Rama that he would keep his waters stable when the monkey brigade crossed the bridge. The sea became still. Then it was time for Rama and the huge army of monkeys to cross the bridge.

Sugreeva said to Rama, "Let Hanuman and Angad carry you and Laxmana on their backs, while the rest of the army walks on." Agreeing to Sugreeva's suggestion, Rama and Laxmana climbed Hanuman and Angad's sturdy shoulders. Once Rama and Laxmana were carried across, the huge battalion of monkeys followed. Some jumped, some screamed, while others danced as they marched on bravely towards Lanka.

# 17 Krishna and Salva

King Salva was upset on hearing about Shishupal's death. He decided to seize the opportunity of Krishna's absence from the city of Dwarka and destroy it.

However, Krishna knew that Shishupal's friends would avenge his death so he rushed back to Dwarka from Hastinapur. On reaching, he found that Salva had already caused a lot of destruction.

Flying his flag atop his chariot, Krishna raced towards the place where Salva was staying.

Seeing the bright flag, Salva's soldiers understood that something was wrong. They immediately gathered their weapons and ran towards the battlefield where the fight between Krishna and Salva had already begun.

Salva fired an arrow that went shooting across the sky, but Krishna shattered it into pieces. Salva flew to the skies and started his attack from there. In return, Krishna shot sixteen arrows one after the other, but the carriage soared higher.

Salva, who was a master magician, then decided to disguise himself as Devaki and fool Krishna. Krishna suddenly saw his mother approaching and with tears rolling down her cheeks she informed Krishna about Vasudeva's death.

Krishna was shocked to hear of his father's death and dropped all his weapons. Seeing Krishna unarmed, Salva again attacked. Krishna was caught unawares, but he quickly rearranged his weapons and resumed the attack.

Finally, Krishna cut off Salva's head with the *Sudarshan Chakra*.

---

# 18 The Hunter's Fast

One day, a hunter named Suswara went hunting to the forest. At nightfall it became very dark so he could not return home. He had to spend the night in the forest. He climbed a bael tree for safety.

That night happened to be Shivaratri. Due to hunger and thirst, he could not sleep all night. He wept thinking about his wife and children. He spent the entire night plucking leaves from the bael tree and throwing them on the ground. When

it was morning he returned home.

Many years passed. At the time of his death, two messengers of Shiva came to take him to heaven. This was because that night of Shivaratri that he had spent in the forest, he had unknowingly worshipped Shiva. There was a *Shivalinga* under the bael tree that he had climbed up. His tears had washed the *Shivalinga* and the bael leaves that he had thrown from the tree had fallen on it. He had even fasted all day and all night.

# 19 Angada Meets Ravana

As Rama's army crossed the bridge to Lanka, he made his last effort to prevent the war. He sent Angada as his messenger to Ravana to convey the message of friendship. Angada said to Ravana, "I have come with the message of friendship. Kindly return our beloved Sita and make peace with the noble Rama." The arrogant Ravana replied, "I will die before making peace with my enemy." Angada answered, "This was your last chance to save yourself, but you chose not to. Now, the mighty Rama will destroy you and your entire kingdom." Ravana seethed with anger as Angada spoke these words. He ordered the *rakshasis* to kill Angada. Two *rakshasis* quickly seized him and were about to drag him away, when Angada, with great force, jumped to the ceiling and escaped.

# 20 Balvala and Balarama

Balvala was a ferocious demon. His hair, beard, and moustache were bright red, while his claw-like teeth were yellow.

Balvala had become a menace to the sages of Naimis-aranya. He used to soil the holy hermitages with blood and defile the sacrificial fire. Tired of this, the sages decided to seek Balarama's help. The sages told him that during the fight, Balarama would come in contact with the demon and therefore he should tour all the holy places to free himself from the impurities of Balvala's body.

Balarama, armed with his plow and club, appeared before Balvala who was flying away on his chariot. Balarama pulled him down with his plow and instantly struck at his head with the club. Balvala's head broke into two.

The inhabitants of Naimis-aranya rejoiced and offered their prayers to Balarama. Meanwhile, the sages prepared for Balarama's holy bath to cleanse the impurities of Balvala's body.

## 21 Ravana Tries to Fool Sita

Ravana wanted to marry Sita and thought that if he could convince Sita of Rama's death, she might agree to marry him.

He went to a *rakshasi* called Vidyut Jibva, and asked her to create a head similar to that of Rama's. Showing Sita the head of Rama, Ravana said, "Look, you foolish woman, my demons have killed Rama. You have to marry me now."

Saying these words, Ravana went back laughing to his palace.

Sita believed Ravana and her heart broke. She wept for Rama, but Trijata consoled her saying that it was just a trick by Ravana. She said she had seen a dream that Rama was approaching Lanka. Sita was overjoyed to hear her words.

## 22 Ravana Joins the Battle

To kill Rama and Laxmana, Ravana sent Prahasta, his most powerful soldier to the battle-field. Unfortunately, he too was killed. Losing all his men one by one, Ravana decided to go to the battlefield himself.

As he arrived with his collection of special weapons, arrows came flying from all directions. Resplendent in his chariot, Ravana positioned himself and started to strike back. Within minutes, he killed hundreds of monkeys. Seeing this, both Rama and Laxmana started firing their weapons at Ravana and gradually weakened him.

The rakshasa king was wounded and his golden crown and his chariot had broken. Without a weapon, Ravana stood helpless on the battle-field. Rama walked up to him and said, "It is not right to fight a soldier when he is unarmed. I shall spare you. Go back and come fully armed tomorrow." Ravana lowered his face in shame and went back to his palace.

## 23 Duryodhana Attacks Viratnagar

When Duryodhana came to know that Kichaka was killed, he was sure that the Pandavas were in Viratnagar because nobody other than Bhima was strong enough to kill him. Duryodhana decided to attack Viratnagar and capture the Pandavas.

Susharma, the ruler of Trigarta, was the enemy of King Virata. He also decided to attack Viratnagar, now that its general was killed. He joined hands with Duryodhana. Both Susharma and Duryodhana attacked Viratnagar from two sides and captured a large territory and cattle. King Virata got frightened. But Yudhisthira offered to help him. Accompanied by the other Pandavas, he fought from King Virata's side. The armies of Susharma and Duryodhana started losing. But Susharma played a trick and captured

Virata. Yudhisthira said to Bhima, "King Virata has given us shelter. It is our duty to protect him." Bhima defeated Susharma and rescued Virata.

Meanwhile, Duryodhana had taken away hundreds of cattle of Viratnagar. Virata sent his son Uttar to fight him. Arjuna, who was working as the royal music teacher, became his charioteer. Faced with the huge army of Duryodhana, Uttar got scared. Seeing this Arjuna

started fighting with Duryodhana. Duryodhana immediately recognised Arjuna and was very happy that the Pandavas were discovered in the thirteenth year of their exile. But Bhishma told him that the thirteenth year was already over. Arjuna bravely fought the Kaurava army and in no time defeated them, freeing all the cattle. When the news of victory reached King Virata, there was jubilation everywhere.

## 24 The End of Kumbhakarna

When Rama spared Ravana for being unarmed, Ravana returned from the battlefield humiliated. Instead of going back himself, he decided to send his brother Kumbhakarna to fight Rama and Laxmana.

Kumbhakarna, who used to sleep for six months at a time, became furious when he was awakened. Ravana explained the urgent situation to him and asked him to leave immediately.

Seeing the gigantic Kumb-

hakarna arrive, the monkeys started fleeing in all directions. Kumbhakarna then grabbed a handful of monkeys and ate them.

Meanwhile, the arrows that Rama and his army fired at Kumbhakarna broke on hitting his strong body.

Finding the arrows ineffective, Rama decided to cut off his head. So he flung his *chakra* and severed the demon's head. The monkeys came back once again and rejoiced on seeing the dead body of the demon.

## 25 Abhimanyu and Uttara

King Virata was very happy to have won the war against Susharma and Duryodhana. He came to know that the five Brahmins who had helped him protect his kingdom were none other than the brave Pandavas. He was very grateful. He also came to know that for one year Arjuna had lived in his palace as a servant where he taught music to his daughter, Uttara. He was overwhelmed with gratitude and said, "Brave Arjuna, please accept my daughter's hand in marriage." Arjuna replied, "I have been your daughter's teacher, I am like her father, I can't marry her. But I will be very happy if you marry her to my brave son, Abhimanyu." King Virata's joy had no bounds. Arjuna called for his son who was at that time in Dwarka.

The wedding was celebrated with great splendour. Abhimanyu's mother, Subhadra; Abhimanyu's uncles, Krishna and Balarama; also graced the occasion.

## 26 Peace Message to Hastinapur

After their exile was over, the Pandavas demanded that Duryodhana give their kingdom back but he simply refused. So a war between the Kauravas and the Pandavas had become necessary. Krishna requested all the kings who were friends of the Pandavas to help them. But Yudhisthira was peace loving. He wanted the dispute to be settled without any war and bloodshed. So Sanjay, the royal priest of King Drupada, Draupadi's father, was sent as a messenger to Hastinapur. Sanjay requested Dhritarashtra to tell Duryodhana to give the Pandavas their kingdom else there would be a war in which the Kauravas were sure to be defeated.

Dhritarashtra, Gandhari, and all the elders of the royal family tried to persuade Duryodhana but he would not listen to anyone.

## 27 The Battle with Meghnad

The famous conflict between Rama and Ravana began at midnight.

At the very beginning, Rama and Laxmana killed six demon chiefs of Ravana. Then they began the search for Ravana's son, Meghnad.

Meghnad had been given the boon of remaining invisible. He started firing arrows at the monkey squad, who failed to discover the source of these attacks. Rama and Laxmana understood that Meghnad was behind these invisible attacks, but before they could do anything, Meghnad took out his famous *Naag paash* weapon and shot at the brothers. This weapon was a huge snake that coiled up like a rope.

As Rama and Laxmana struggled to get out of the wrap, Meghnad shot several snake arrows at the brothers. These arrows pierced their bodies and made them unconscious.

Seeing Rama and Laxmana almost dead, Meghnad rushed to his father's court to give him the news.

## 28 Bholu and the Princess

Betal narrated another story as Vikram carried him.

In King Kiripal's kingdom, there lived a big giant who used to eat people. The king said that whoever killed the giant would marry the princess as a reward. Many people tried but were eaten up by the demon. One day, an ordinary village boy, Bholu, killed the giant. But the king did not want to marry his daughter to him. He said that Bholu had to pass a test before he could get the reward. But Bholu refused the reward. However, the princess declared that she would marry Bholu.

Betal asked Vikram, "Why did they do that?" Vikram replied, "Bholu declined the reward because he killed the giant for the welfare of people. The princess wanted to marry Bholu to keep her father's word." Betal heard this and flew away.

## 29  The Right Suitor

Betal narrated another story to Vikram. Three men Mohan, Sohan, and Rohan loved a girl named Manju. But before she could choose anyone of them, she died. The men decided to devote their lives to her memory. Mohan started living near river Ganga. Sohan always kept Manju's ashes with him. Rohan started staying with a Brahmin. One day, the Brahmin's wife died. The Brahmin put some water from the Ganga on his wife's ashes and chanted a mantra. His wife became alive.

Rohan watched the whole incident. He learnt the mantra and decided to bring Manju back to life. Sohan brought Manju's ashes, Mohan put water from the Ganga on her and Rohan chanted the mantra. Thus, Manju came back to life. Betal asked Vikram, "Whom should Manju marry?" Vikram replied, "Manju should marry Sohan because if he had not kept the ashes, the mantra could not bring her back to life." Hearing this, Betal flew away.

## 30  Karna's Promise

The war between the Kauravas and Pandavas had become necessary.

Kunti was very disturbed by this. She went to Karna and said, "Karna, you are actually my son. If you fight against the Pandavas, you will be fighting against your own brothers. You should join the Pandavas in the war." Karna replied, "I knew that you are my real mother but you had given me up when I was only a baby; I was brought up by a charioteer. It was Duryodhana who made me the king of Anga. I am grateful to him and can't betray him. I will fight against the Pandavas."

Hearing this Kunti was upset and started weeping. Karna was moved and could not see his mother like that and said, "But I can promise you one thing, that I will not harm any of the Pandavas except Arjuna who is my rival."

# 31 Grushmeshwar

Once, many years ago, in the southern part of the country, there lived a Brahmin, Sudharma, who lived happily with his wife Sudeha. But unfortunately, they were childless. This made Sudeha very upset and forlorn. When Sudeha came to know that she could never give birth to a child, she asked Gruhshma, her sister, to marry Sudharma so that she could bear him a child instead.

Gruhsuma agreed and the Brahmin and his two wives lived very happily. Gruhshma was a devotee of Shiva. Every day she made one hundred and one *lingas* and floated them in the nearby pond. Eventually, Gruhshma gave birth to a baby boy. The family now lived very peacefully with all their wishes granted. Meanwhile, Sudeha became jealous of Gruhshma and her son.

One day, Sudeha killed Gruhshma's son and dumped his body in the pond. The next morning, when everybody discovered the death of the young boy, everyone was very upset and grieved for him. However, Gruhshma calmly performed her daily ritual of floating the *lingas* in the pond. As soon as she did that, her son emerged from the pond and walked towards her safe and alive.

Shiva also appeared. He was very angry and wanted to punish Sudeha for attempting to kill the little child but Gruhshma begged him to forgive her sister. On Gruhshma's request, Shiva became the *Jyotirling Grushmeshwar* and stayed there.

# Contents

*The Story of the Month: Nala and Damayanti*

The Story of the Month

# Nala and Damayanti

# Nala and Damayanti

King Nishadh of Ayodhya had two sons Nala and Kuvara. Nala wanted to marry Damayanti, the beautiful daughter of King Bhima. Damayanti did not know him, so Nala sent his swan to her. The swan flew to Damayanti's palace and finding her alone in the garden, sang praises of Nala. Meanwhile, King Bhima arranged for her *swayamvara*, where many princes gathered from whom Damayanti could chose her husband. Damayanti chose Nala and they got married.

When King Nishadh died, Nala became king. He conquered many other kingdoms and became famous. This made his brother Kuvara jealous. He knew that gambling was Nala's weakness. Kuvara challenged Nala to a game of dice in which Nala lost everything. Kuvara became the king and banished Nala from his kingdom. Nala went to the forest and Damayanti, who loved him very much followed him. As they walked in the forest, Damayanti injured her feet. Nala did not want the delicate Damayanti to go through hardships with him, so when she was sleeping he left her and went ahead. Further into the forest, he found a snake on the top of a tree that had caught fire from below. As he tried to bring it down, the snake bit him and Nala turned dark and developed a hunchback. Nala asked the snake, "Why did you bite me? I was trying to save your life." The snake said, "I am your father Nishadh. The next twelve years will be full of difficulties for you. I changed your appearance to protect you from your enemies. Whenever you want to get back your original looks wear this ornament."

Nala proceeded to another kingdom. Meanwhile, when Damayanti woke up she found a note from Nala asking her to go to her parents. As she moved ahead, she met a demon that threatened to eat her.

Impressed with her fearlessness he came into his real form. He was actually a god, who told her that she would unite with her husband after twelve years. Damayanti proceeded to Achalpura kingdom where she became the queen's maid. Nala went to the kingdom of Sumsumara and became a servant of the king. Many years passed.

One day, King Bhima's men found Damayanti in Achalpura and brought her back to her father. King Bhima tried to find Nala but failed, so he made a plan. He arranged the *swayamvara* of Damayanti knowing that when Nala came to know about the second marriage of his wife, he would certainly come to her. King Bhima was right. Nala came with his master, the king of Samsumara. A day before the *swayamvara* Damayanti saw the dark hunchback servant. She immediately recognised him. Nala also put on the ornament given by his father and regained his original looks. But the *swayamvara* had been arranged so Damayanti asked him to be present there. On the day of *swayamvara* she put the garland around Nala's neck and they were united. The twelve-year period was also over. With the help of King Bhima's army, Nala won his kingdom back and again became the king of Ayodhya.

One day, a monk visited Nala's palace and told him the reason why he had to undergo the twelve-year exile. In their previous birth also Nala and Damayanti were king and queen and they had thrown an innocent monk in prison. Their exile was a punishment for their karma of a previous birth.

Eventually, Nala and Damayanti had a son Pushkara. After making him the king, they renounced the world in search of spiritual enlightenment.

# 1 The Noble Robber

Betal narrated another story while Vikram was carrying him.

Anand was a minister in the king's court. He loved a girl called Anju. But when he came to know that Anju's marriage had already been arranged with someone else, he was disappointed and decided never to marry.

When Anju came to know about Anand's pledge, she wrote him a letter saying that she would come to meet him after her wedding. On her wedding night, she told her husband about Anand and went to his house. On the way, a robber tried to take her jewels away. She told him that she would return after a while and he could take her jewellery then. The robber let her go.

When Anand saw Anju he thought that if he accepted another man's wife, the king would punish him. So he asked her to return to her husband.

Anju decided to go back to her husband. On the way, she met the robber and told him her story. She even offered him her jewels. The robber was good at heart. He did not accept the jewels and escorted Anju to her house. When Anju went back to her husband, he refused to accept her. With nowhere to go, Anju killed herself.

Betal asked Vikram, "Who was the only noble man among the three?" Vikram replied, "The robber was the only noble man because he helped a girl in trouble at a time when he could have easily robbed her." Betal heard this and flew away since Vikram had spoken aloud.

# 2 Krishna's Peace Mission

When Sanjay failed to convince Duryodhana to come to a compromise with the Pandavas and prevent a battle, Krishna decided to go to Hastinapur himself as a messenger of the Pandavas and persuade Duryodhana.

Krishna was given a warm welcome at the court. Krishna said to Duryodhana, "I have come with an offer from the Pandavas. Instead of returning their whole kingdom, they would settle for just five villages because they are peace loving and want to prevent war."

Duryodhana scornfully replied, "The whole kingdom belongs to me. I will not even give land equal to the tip of a needle from my kingdom to the Pandavas. You are always partial to those Pandavas. I will imprison you." He ordered his soldiers to imprison Krishna.

Krishna came to his cosmic form (*virata roopa*). Everybody was scared to see this. Then Krishna left the court.

## 3 Preparations for the War

After meeting Duryodhana, Krishna returned to the Pandavas and told them to prepare for war, as Duryodhana was not ready for a settlement. A meeting of all the kings who were ready to support the Pandavas was called. The Pandavas divided their army into seven regiments. Each regiment was placed under an efficient commander. These were Drupada, Virata, Shikhandi, Chekitana, Bhimasena, Satyaki, and Dhrishtadyumna. Dhrishtadyumna was the commander-in-chief. On the Kaurava side, there were warriors like Bhishma, Dronacharya, and Kripacharya. Bhishma agreed to become the commander-in-chief on the condition that he would not kill the Pandavas, only fight with them and that as long as he would fight in the war, Karna would not fight.

## 4 Sakhubai's Devotion

Sakhubai was born into a very poor family of Pandharpur. She was a great devotee of Panduranga Vittala, which is another name of Krishna.

She was married into a rich family but her in-laws were very cruel. They beat her up, gave her leftover food to eat, and took away all her jewellery.

Sakhubai bore all the pain and asked Vittala to give her strength. She dearly wished to see him. Vittala gave her a vision that would help her to see him.

One day, Vittala in the guise of a woman told Sakhubai to go to Pandharpur to see the Lord. He took the place of Sakhubai in her house and worked tirelessly. Meanwhile, Sakhubai forgot everything in her devotion to God. She breathed her last while praying. Seeing her devotion Krishna brought her back to life. When Sakhubai came back and narrated the truth to her in-laws they repented misbehaving with her.

## 5 Kedarnath

After winning the war, the Pandavas went on a pilgrimage to Mount Kailash. They wanted Shiva to cleanse them of the sin of killing so many people. When Shiva saw them he hid. When they couldn't find him, Yudhisthira said, "I know you have hidden because we have sinned, but we will not leave without seeing you." As they moved ahead, a bull attacked them. Bhima started fighting it. The bull hid his head within a crack in a rock. Bhima tried to pull him out by his tail, but the body of the bull got separated from his head. The body turned into a *Shivalinga* from which Shiva appeared and forgave them their sins.

The *linga* is still present in the Himalayas and is called Kedarnath.

## 6 A Father's Love

Betal put forward another puzzle to Vikram. A woman called Leelavati married a thief. After marriage the man decided to quit stealing. However, when they had a son, the man found he had no money to support his family and went back to stealing. After his death, Leelavati married a businessman.

The businessman loved his family and raised the child well. Just when the boy took charge of the business, his parents died.

While performing their last rites in the river, three hands came out claiming the offering. The boy recognised his mother's voice and offered prayers to her, but he couldn't make out which pair of hand was his father's. At this point he recalled his mother once mentioning his real father.

Betal stopped the story here and asked which father was finally given the offering.

"The businessman," replied Vikram. "Because he had showered his love and reared the child, while the thief had only given him birth." Again, Betal flew away.

## 7  Arjuna and Duryodhana go to Krishna

As the preparations for the war were being made, both the Kauravas and the Pandavas were trying to get the support of more and more kings from far and wide.

Duryodhana went to Krishna, the king of Dwarka, to ask for his support. He reached Krishna's palace, but at that time Krishna was taking a nap. So Duryodhana went and took a seat beside his head and waited for him to wake up. At the same time, Arjuna also came to Krishna to ask him to support the Pandavas in the war. Arjuna was very humble and sat near Krishna's feet.

When Krishna woke up, he saw Arjuna first because Duryodhana was sitting behind him. Duryodhana said, "I have come to ask for your support in the war." Arjuna also made the same request. Duryodhana said, "I came before Arjuna, so you should help me and not him." Krishna said, "Due to your pride you sat beside my head so I saw Arjuna first. But you are both dear to me so I will help you both. To one of you I will give my army (Narayani Sena) and to the other I will give my moral support because I will not fight in the war. Arjuna is younger so I will ask him to choose."

Arjuna, without wasting a second, chose Krishna's moral support. He knew that with his support and guidance, the Pandavas would certainly win the war.

When Duryodhana heard Arjuna's choice, he was very happy. He was foolish enough to think that Krishna, who wouldn't even fight in the war, would be of no use to him; Krishna's huge army would certainly be of help.

## 8  Code of War

On the eve of the war of Kurukshetra, Krishna and the Pandavas made plans for the war. On the other side, Bhishma discussed his plans with Duryodhana.

On the day of the war, both the armies stood face to face in the field of Kurukshetra. Both sides finalised the six codes of the war and pledged to abide by it.

First, there would be no war at night, it would be suspended at sunset daily; second, the fight would be fair; third, no unarmed soldier would be attacked; fourth, no soldier who has accepted his defeat would be attacked; fifth, the soldiers who would be carrying the war-material would not be attacked; and finally, the camps where wounded soldiers would be kept would not be attacked. The commanders of both the sides encouraged their soldiers to fight till their last breath. The soldiers were told that a warrior either returns victorious or falls fighting.

# 9 The Bhagavad Gita

As the two armies stood face-to-face on the battlefield, Arjuna suddenly looked at the opponents and realised that he was up against the people whom he loved and respected the most—Bhishma, Dronacharya, and Kripacharya. Even if he won, his victory would be sad. With all these doubts in mind, he put his bow and arrow down. Krishna, who was not only Arjuna's charioteer but also his guide, understood what Arjuna was thinking. He delivered a sermon on Karma, and the immortality of the soul. He told Arjuna that the one who dies fighting, loses his temporary body but his soul finds a seat in heaven. He told that it was Arjuna's duty to fight. This sermon became renowned as the Bhagavad Gita. Hearing this, Arjuna's doubts were removed and he was ready for battle.

# 10 Yudhisthira Seeks Blessings

As the Kaurava and Pandava armies stood face-to-face, ready for the attack, there was sudden uproar in the Pandava army. Everybody was surprised to see that Yudhisthira had placed all his weapons on the ground and was moving towards the Kauravas. Arjuna and Krishna ran behind him fearing that Yudhisthira might call off the war. Yudhisthira went through the Kaurava army to the place where Bhishma was standing on his chariot. He touched Bhishma's feet and said, "We are being forced to fight against you because of the stubbornness of Duryodhana. I request your permission to fight and your blessings." Bhishma was overjoyed. He permitted Yudhisthira to fight and blessed him. Then Yudhisthira went to Dronacharya, Kripacharya, and his maternal uncle Shalya for their blessings. All of them blessed Yudhisthira.

# 11 Laxmana Becomes Unconscious

Meghnad, Ravana's son, was determined to kill Rama and Laxmana. When he entered the battlefield, Laxmana started shooting arrows at him. Soon, Laxmana destroyed Meghnad's chariot and even killed his charioteer. Meghnad was furious and shot a *brahmaastra* at Laxmana. As soon as the dreadful arrow hit Laxmana, he fell unconscious. Rama rushed to his beloved brother and tried to revive him.

# 12 The War Begins

With the resounding of the conch shells, the Mahabharata war began. Soldiers armed with different weapons ran towards each other. Bhishma attacked the army with such might that the Pandava soldiers shuddered out of fear. Abhimanyu, the son of Arjuna and Subhadra, was given the responsibility of facing Bhishma. He showered a volley of arrows on him. In retaliation, the Kaurava warriors surrounded Abhimanyu from all sides. But brave Abhimanyu fought with unflinching courage. Other Pandava warriors came to help him and the Kauravas had to step back. The first day ended with a lot of casualties on both sides. But the Pandava army suffered major setbacks due to the death of Utar and Shweta, the two princes of Viratnagar. But both the warriors fell fighting after killing hundreds of Kaurava soldiers.

# 13 Bhimeshwar

Bhima was the son of demon Kumbhakarna. When he came to know that Rama had killed his father, he wanted to take revenge. He performed *tapasya* for one year and pleased Brahma who gave him many boons. He captured heaven and earth. He banned all kinds of worship on earth. Those who tried to worship gods were imprisoned. He also imprisoned Shiva's devotee Sudakshina. All the gods went to Shiva and asked him to kill Bhima. One day, Sudhakshina made a *Shivalinga* in the prison and started worshipping it. When Bhima came to know about this he went to the prison and struck the *Shivalinga* with a sword. Out came Shiva himself and burnt Bhima with one blow of his breath. The *Shivalinga* was called Bhimeshwar and is still worshipped.

# 14 The Reformed Dacoit

Betal narrated another story while Vikram was carrying him.

Once, there lived a gang of robbers in a forest. Their leader was Ugrasen, who was very cruel. They used to loot the nearby villages. After some years, Ugrasen's wife gave birth to a baby boy. Ugrasen loved him very much and played with him all the time. Slowly his heart began to soften. One night, he dreamt that the king's soldiers had killed him and his son was orphaned. When he woke up he was reformed and decided to surrender. The other dacoits did not like this idea and threatened to kill his wife and son. Ugrasen fled with his wife and son and went to the king. The king forgave him.

Betal asked Vikram, "Was the king right in forgiving Ugrasen?" Vikram replied, "Yes, Ugrasen had surrendered on his own. This shows that he was reformed." Betal heard this and flew away since once again, Vikram had spoken aloud.

# 15 Bhishma Falls

During the Mahabharata war there was fierce fighting for nine days. On the tenth day, Arjuna and Bhishma came face-to-face. Arjuna showered arrows on Bhishma, which pierced every inch of his body. Bhishma fell on the ground, his body supported by arrows. Bhishma lay on a bed of arrows with his head hanging down. Arjuna shot three arrows to support Bhishma's hanging head. The dying Bhishma told Arjuna, that he was thirsty. Arjuna shot an arrow to the ground and a fountain of water gushed out of it that reached Bhishma's mouth.

Bhishma blessed Arjuna. He called Duryodhana and warned him for the last time to come to a settlement with the Pandavas. Karna also came to pay homage to Bhishma and begged pardon for his past misconduct. The fall of Bhishma marked the beginning of the defeat of the Kauravas.

## 16 Hanuman Saves Laxmana

When Laxmana fell unconscious during the battle with Ravana, following Jambavan's orders, Hanuman flew to the Himalayas. He landed on a peak between the Kailasa and Rishabha mountains. There, Hanuman began searching for the *sanjeevani* herb, but since he had no knowledge of herbs he stood confused thinking what to do. An idea dawned on him. He uprooted the whole mountain and holding it in one hand flew back to Lanka.

Everyone was surprised to *see* Hanuman approach with the gigantic mountain on his hand. Quickly Jambavan plucked the *sanjeevani* and ground it into a juice. As the juice trickled into Laxmana's mouth, he regained his senses. Rama heaved a sigh of relief. Meanwhile the other monkeys gathered around Hanuman; some admired him; some felt his muscles while others stood startled. Impressed with Hanuman's effort the gods hailed him and showered their blessings on him.

## 17 Krishna and Sudama

Sudama was Krishna's friend and devotee. He belonged to a poor Brahmin family. Years passed and Krishna became king of Dwarka but Sudama remained a poor man. Sudama and his wife and children starved without food.

Tired of their pitiable state, one day his wife advised him to seek his friend Krishna's help. Sudama who was an extremely honest man felt ashamed to ask for help. When his wife insisted, Sudama agreed to go, but realised that going empty-handed to meet a friend after so long would look odd. So he carried with him a handful of puffed rice as a gift.

Krishna greeted Sudama warmly when he arrived at the palace. Seeing the splendour of Dwarka, Sudama felt awed. Krishna's hospitality humbled him, and he was now feeling embarrassed to take out his simple gift. Seeing a small bag in Sudama's hand, Krishna promptly asked him whether his gift was inside the bag. Sudama unwillingly took it out and said he could not gift a handful of puffed rice to a king. Krishna immediately understood Sudama's problem. He happily accepted the gift as if it was the most precious thing.

When Sudama reached home the next day, he saw a huge mansion instead of his hut and his family wearing new clothes. He went inside and found lots of food. At once he knew that God had showered his blessings on him.

# 18 The Fussy Brothers

Vikram ran to the tree and pulled Betal down. As he began to carry Betal, Betal began narrating another story.

Once there were two brothers who were very fussy. The first brother Gopal was fussy about his food; the second one Deepak was fussy about where he slept. Gopal would eat only very good and selective food and Deepak could sleep only on a very comfortable bed.

Their fussiness was so famous that one day the king called them to find out who was fussier of the two. Gopal was given the best quality rice to eat. But he refused to eat it saying that the rice smelled of a cremation ground. On investigation it was found out that the rice actually was grown on a field next to a cremation ground.

When it was Deepak's turn,

he was given a bed with seven soft mattresses on it. But he could not sleep all night. In the morning he had a rash on his back. He said that there was something under the mattresses. On investigation it was found that there was a hair under the seventh mattress.

Betal asked Vikram, "Who was the fussier among the two brothers?"

Vikram replied, "Deepak was

fussier because the rash was a physical proof of his discomfort. While there was no such proof in the case of Gopal. Who knows he could have asked someone about the rice?"

Betal was surprised and said, "How do you manage to give the correct answer to every question I ask? But you opened your mouth, so here I go." Saying so, Betal flew back to the tree.

# 19 Dronacharya Becomes the Commander-in-Chief

After the fall of Bhishma, Duryodhana wanted Karna to be the next commander-in-chief. He knew that Karna was capable of defeating Arjuna and asked him to take charge of the army. However, Karna asked Duryodhana to make Drona the commander-in-chief as this would be acceptable to everyone. Duryodhana liked the idea and Dronacharya was made the commander-in-chief. The Kaurava army got a new breath of

life because they were sure that the brave guru would lead them to victory. Karna had pledged that he would not fight under Drona, so he left the battlefield. But Drona requested him to forget all grudges and join the battle for the sake of his friend, Duryodhana. To everybody's joy, Karna agreed and joined the battle. Duryodhana knew that Drona would never kill any of the Pandavas so he asked him to capture Yudhisthira alive. Drona did not mind carrying out this order and rearranged the army to achieve this end.

## 20 The End of Meghnad

After a terrible battle when Ravana realised that Rama and Laxmana were still alive, he once again appealed to Meghnad. With magical power Meghnad launched an attack from his flying chariot. Hundreds of monkeys died on the spot. Then he decided to create some illusory trick. He created a replica of Sita and cut off her head. Rama was devastated to hear the news. Vibhisana explained to him that this was just another trick. After this Meghnad began his *yajna* to gain immortality and the weapon, Brahmasir. Furious Rama sent Laxmana to the battlefield armed with the *Indraastra*. Meghnad's *yajna* to gain immortality remained incomplete. Then climbing on Hanuman's shoulders Laxmana launched the *Indraastra* at Meghnad and killed him.

## 21 The Broken Code of War

During the battle, Drona had been ordered to capture Yudhisthira alive, so Arjuna always protected him. Once Arjuna had gone after the Kaurava warriors and Yudhisthira was unprotected. Drona approached Yudhisthira with his soldiers arranged in the circular formation known as *chakravyuh*. Arjun's son, Abhimanyu, had learnt from his father how to enter the *chakravyuh* but did not know how to come out of it. Only Arjuna knew how to break the *chakravyuh*. But, Abhimanyu decided to enter the formation.

Jaidhratha, the king of Sindhudesha, had obtained a boon from Shiva that he would be able to stop the Pandavas for one day. He stopped them from entering the *chakravyuh* to help Abhimanyu. Six warriors including Drona, Duryodhana, and Karna together attacked Abhimanyu. He lost all his weapons. Finally, the Kaurava warriors broke the code of war; they attacked the unarmed Abhimanyu and killed him.

## 22 The End of Jaidratha

Arjuna came to know that his son, Abhimanyu, had been killed against the code of war. He was told that Jaidratha was responsible for it. Arjuna was grief-stricken and furious. He took a vow—either he would end Jaidratha's life before the sun set on the fourteenth day or kill himself. On the fourteenth day the Kaurava army was so arranged as to protect Jaidratha. But Arjuna cut through the array of soldiers and reached Jaidratha. But just as he was going to kill him, there was darkness. The Kauravas were happy that the sun had set and Arjuna would now have to kill himself. Arjuna was sorrowful, but Krishna told Arjuna to be ready. The sun reappeared for a few minutes and Arjuna killed Jaidratha.

## 23 The Fall of Drona

The fourteenth day of the battle of Kurukshetra was drawing to a close. Drona was unhappy because neither could he capture Yudhisthira nor could he save Jaidrath. So he attacked the Pandava soldiers with more force than ever. Krishna told the Pandavas that Drona could be killed by a trick. Krishna asked the Pandavas to spread the false news that Drona's son, Ashwatthama, had been killed. Bhima killed an elephant named Ashvatthama and shouted, "I have killed Ashvatthama." When Drona heard this, he was full of sorrow. He asked Yudhisthira whether it was true; he knew that Yudhisthira would never lie. Yudhisthira replied, "Yes, Ashvatthama is dead, but the elephant not your son." But Krishna asked the drummers to beat the drums when Yudhisthira spoke the last part of the sentence, so Drona couldn't hear it. He sat mourning his son's death and Dhrishtadyumna who had been born to kill Drona, cut his head off.

## 24 Ravana Is Killed by Rama

The joyous shouts of Rama's army was enough to convince Ravana of his son Meghnad's death. Breaking down in his huge chamber, Ravana felt defeat was already his, yet he had to fight on. Lonely, he prepared for the bloody battle ahead. Ravana mounted his chariot and went charging to the battlefield.

At once Ravana fired his fearful arrows at Laxmana, and made him unconscious. Finally, he stood face to face with Rama. While both were equal in strength and bravery, one was virtuous, the other evil. The gods anxiously watched to see the outcome of this legendary fight.

Ravana looked fearsome with his ten heads and twenty arms. Rama shot one arrow after another to cut off his heads, but after every shot they would grow back again. He was awestruck. He then shot another series of arrows at Ravana, but he laughed seeing them.

Rama grew anxious. The gods who were watching from above asked Indra to help. Indra sent his celestial chariot driven by Matali to help Rama. As the chariot descended on earth, Rama quickly climbed it and started firing weapons.

Matali then asked Rama to use the *brahmashastra*. Rama took up the weapon, chanted Parvati's name and aimed it at Ravana's heart. The potent weapon pierced his body and Ravana fell dead.

Loud cheers echoed through Lanka. Flowers were showered from the heavens above. The gods announced the end of Ravana. Vibhisana refused to do the last rites, but Rama explained that he was after all a brother and had died like a warrior too. So Ravana deserved a proper funeral.

## 25 Karna Meets His End

After the fall of Drona, Karna assumed command of the Kaurava army during the battle of Kurukshetra. On the fifteenth day, Arjuna and Karna came face to face. A fast and furious battle took place between the famous rivals. One of Karna's arrows almost hit Arjuna, but Krishna, who was Arjuna's charioteer, lowered the chariot and the arrow missed him. In return, Arjuna shot numerous arrows at him. Suddenly, the wheel of Karna's chariot got stuck in the mud. He got down to push the wheel and asked Arjuna to stop shooting, because it would not be fair to shoot at him while he pushed the wheel out of the mud. Krishna said, "You shot at the unarmed Abhimanyu. Was that fair?" Krishna then reminded Arjuna how the Kauravas had broken the code of war when they killed Abhimanyu without mercy. He told Arjuna to do his duty. Hearing this Arjuna was filled with righteous anger and killed Karna.

## 26 Shakuni Meets His End

Shakuni was Duryodhana's wicked uncle who had helped the Kauravas win the Pandavas' half of the kingdom from them in a game of dice, and sent them into exile. He was very cunning and devious. On the sixteenth day of the battle of Kurukshetra, a fierce fight was going on between Nakula and Shakuni. Shakuni was a brave warrior and he was overpowering Nakula, when Nakula's brother, Sahadeva, came to his rescue. He shot an arrow at Shakuni saying, "It is your evil mind and numerous sins that have led to this war. Now face your doom." The arrow cut Shakuni's head off.

After Shakuni's death, Duryodhana was left all alone. He did not even have Karna to support him. Duryodhana realised that his end was also near and was sad and broken-hearted.

## 27 Rama Meets Sita

Rama sent Hanuman to fetch Sita from Vatika.

When she arrived before Rama, tears of joy rolled down her cheeks and she ran to embrace him, but Rama stopped her.

Rama too was delighted to meet Sita after so long. He told her that he and Laxmana had risked their lives to save her. He said, "I have risked everything to save you. For the past one year you have lived in another man's house. You have to prove your purity."

Hearing this Sita asked Laxmana to set up her funeral pyre. Laxmana looked at Rama, but the latter was unmoved. He had no choice but to obey Sita's order.

As the flames rose up, Sita mounted the pyre, but miraculously did not burn. Rama and Sita were reunited again and all the gods in the heavens blessed them.

## 28 Vibhisana's Coronation

After years of unrest, it was now time to place a just ruler on the throne of Lanka. The head priests recited hymns as Rama placed the jewelled crown on Vibhisana's head. Sugreeva, Laxmana, and Hanuman looked on as the people of Lanka cheered for their new king. Vibhisana received many gifts during the coronation, but he gave them all to Rama as a token of appreciation.

## 29 Gandhari Tries to Protect Her Son

Gandhari and Kunti had reached Kurukshetra. Gandhari was worried about Duryodhana as he was her only son who was alive. She had come up with a plan to keep him alive. She asked him to take a bath and appear naked in front of her. She would open the cloth over her eyes and cast a look on his body. By the power of her prayers nobody could hurt his body. No amount of Bhima's mace blows would be able to hurt his body. Krishna came to know about Gandhari's plan.

Duryodhana followed his mother's advice, and was going to his mother after a bath. Krishna stopped him and made fun of him saying, "How can you go to your mother looking like that?" Duryodhana felt ashamed and wrapped a cloth around his waist. When he appeared before his mother, his entire body became solid except his thighs.

## 30 Indra Grants Rama a Wish

During the terrible war between Rama and Ravana, Indra appeared before Rama and said the gods were happy with Rama and he would grant any wish that Rama wanted. Rama said he was unhappy to see the destruction wrought on Sugreeva's army and added that he wanted all the monkeys to be brought back to life. He also begged for the place of their dwelling to be always filled with trees and fruits.

Indra agreed and sent his blessings on the battlefield where all the monkeys lay dead. One by one these monkeys regained their lives. The other monkeys were awestruck to see this miracle. Then Indra and the other gods asked Rama to return to Ayodhya and accept its kingship. So Rama, Laxmana, and Sita bid a tearful goodbye and left for Ayodhya.

# Contents

The Story of the Month
# Upmanyu

# Upmanyu

The great sage Ayodhdhaumya had many disciples, but a young boy called Upmanyu was his favourite. One day, the sage decided to test Upmanyu's devotion and asked him, "You look very healthy, what do you eat?" In those days, sages and their disciples used to beg for food and alms. Upmanyu calmly replied, "I eat the food that I get by begging." On hearing this, the sage instructed Upmanyu not to consume any food that he received as alms without asking for his permission first. Upmanyu was very obedient and from the next day itself, he offered everything that he

received to the sage. The sage took away all the food and gave nothing to Upmanyu.

After a few days, the sage noticed that Upmanyu still looked very healthy. The sage then asked him, "I take away all the food that you get, so what do you eat?" Upmanyu explained that he offered the sage everything that he received the first time he went begging, and that he ate what he got the second time he went begging. The sage scolded Upmanyu and ordered, "You should not beg twice, because then there will be nothing left for other students. You should

not be greedy." Upmanyu obediently followed what his teacher said.

After some days, the saint noticed that Upmanyu still looked hale and hearty and asked him, "You still look healthy, what do you eat these days?" Upmanyu replied saying, "When I take the cows out to graze, I drink some of the milk that they give." The sage immediately forbade Upmanyu from having milk from the cows. As usual, Upmanyu followed his teacher's instructions.

However, Upmanyu's health still did not suffer. The sage approached him again after a few days and asked him what he ate. Upmanyu promptly

replied that he ate the foam that the calves produced after having milk from the cows. The sage told Upmanyu that this would affect the health of the calves and he should not do so. Upmanyu followed Ayodhdhaumya's advice.

The next day, when Upmanyu took the cows for grazing as usual, he felt very hungry. When he couldn't control his hunger anymore, he ate the leaves of a plant called *Aak*. The leaves of this plant were very poisonous and Upmanyu became blind. He kept wandering in the forest and then fell into a dry

well. When Upmanyu did not return in the evening, the sage was worried and went with his disciples to look for Upmanyu. They found Upmanyu in the well and pulled him out. When the sage heard how Upmanyu had been blinded, he asked him to pray to the Ashwini Kumars, the doctors of the gods, and request them to restore his eyesight. Soon, the Ashwini Kumars appeared and gave Upmanyu a medicine. Upmanyu refused the medicine and said that he would not eat anything without Ayodhdhaumya's

permission. The Ashwini Kumars tried their best to convince Upmanyu to have the medicine but Upmanyu said that he would rather stay blind forever than disobey the orders of the sage.

The gods were impressed by Upmanyu's love, respect, and devotion for his teacher and blessed him. They restored his eyesight. Ayodhdhaumya was also very pleased with Upmanyu and told him that he had passed the test. The sage blessed Upmanyu and gave him a boon that he wouldn't need to learn religious texts but would know them automatically.

# 1 The Flying Machine

Once Betal joked, "Vikram, I think you need a flying machine to catch me." Saying this he began narrating a story about a flying machine.

A girl called Chandraprabha had decided to marry a great scholar, a warrior, or an inventor. Her family began searching for grooms to fit her choice. Her father met a warrior who had won many medals for his show of courage. Impressed, he promised to marry his daughter to the warrior. At the same time, her brother met a brilliant scholar and her mother an inventor, and both offered Chandraprabha's hand.

One day, all the three suitors decided to meet Chandraprabha. While the warrior and the scholar came walking, the inventor flew down in his newly made flying machine. An argument started among

the father, the brother, and the mother as to which man among the three was the best. Suddenly, they heard loud screams and rushed to see what had happened. They found a huge demon speeding away with Chandraprabha on the flying machine.

While Chandraprabha's parents panicked, the scholar and the inventor stood watching helplessly. The warrior attacked the demon with his sword and saved her. Now Chandraprabha wondered which suitor to choose.

So Betal asked Vikram, "Which man did Chandraprabha finally marry?" Vikram said, "The warrior, because he risked his life to save her while the other two did nothing." Hearing the answer, Betal flew away like the flying machine.

# 2 Rama Returns to Ayodhya

After killing Ravana and rescuing Sita, Rama, Laxmana, and Sita made preparations for their return to Ayodhya. They sat in a flying chariot and bid farewell to the army of monkeys. However, the monkeys insisted on accompanying Rama so he decided to take them along. Meanwhile, Rama sent Hanuman to Ayodhya to let everyone know that they were all returning.

The entire city of Ayodhya was brightly lit and people thronged the roads with garlands in their hands to welcome Rama. As soon as the flying chariot touched the ground, Bharata rushed forward to touch Rama and Sita's feet. Rama, Laxmana, and Sita met their mothers, Kaushalya, Sumitra, and Kaikeyi, who was very ashamed of her deeds.

Sage Vashishta ordered arrangements for Rama's coronation to be made. Finally, Rama sat on the throne and Sage Vashishta crowned him the king of Ayodhya and the other sages also blessed him. The people of Ayodhya rejoiced.

# 3 Bhima Takes Revenge

After Gandhari had blessed Duryodhana with the boon that no one could harm him with a mace, Duryodhana went and hid in a lake of water fearing that the Pandavas would come to kill him. When the Pandavas saw him, they challenged him to come out of hiding. Yudhisthira asked him which of the Pandavas he would like to fight with and with what weapon. Duryodhana chose the mace and opted to fight with Bhima.

Although Bhima was stronger, Duryodhana was more skilled at handling a mace. The duel went on and on. Finally, Krishna touched his thigh and gave a signal to Bhima to strike Duryodhana on his thighs. Bhima promptly hit Duryodhana hard on his thighs. Duryodhana fell to the ground and the Pandavas left him there to die a painful death.

# 4 The True Devotee

Hanuman was a loyal follower of Rama and worshipped him wholeheartedly. One day, Sita gave him a precious pearl necklace. Hanuman immediately broke the necklace and started looking at each pearl carefully. He glared at each pearl and threw them away, one by one, in disgust. Sita was surprised and asked him for an explanation.

Hanuman explained that he was looking for Rama's image in the pearls. Hanuman believed that Rama was present everywhere and was disappointed that he could not find his image in the pearls. He declared the pearls were just stones and pebbles and thus, were worthless. When the people around him asked if Rama was present in Hanuman, Hanuman tore open his chest with his hands and everyone was amazed to see a brilliant image of Rama and Sita engraved in his heart.

The people accepted that Hanuman was a true devotee of Rama. This is why he is also known as Bhakta Hanuman.

## 5 Ashvattama's Plan

When Dronacharya's son, Ashvattama, came to know that Duryodhana was dying, he was furious and vowed that he would kill the Pandavas. Ashvattama devised an evil plan. He took two warriors and went to the camp of the Pandavas' army at night. First, he went to Draupadi's brother, Dhristadhyumna and strangled him while he was sleeping. Then, one by one, he killed all the five sons of Draupadi and finally, Shikhandi, Draupadi's elder brother. Then he set fire to the camp and quickly left. Next morning, the Pandavas were shocked to see what had happened the night before. Draupadi was devastated. Meanwhile, Ashvattama rushed to Duryodhana to inform him of his success. Duryodhana was pleased and breathed his last.

## 6 Rama Kills Shambuk

One day, an old Brahmin walked into Rama's court with the dead body of his son. He was crying and started blaming Rama for the death of his five-year-old son. The Brahmin said that he had never committed a sin in his life and couldn't understand why his son had died at such an early age. He was convinced that his son must have died as a result of some sins committed by Rama.

Rama was very sad and summoned Sage Vashishtha. The sage told him that a man called Shambuk, an untouchable, was doing a very powerful *tapasya*, which he was not permitted to do. If he was punished, the little boy would come back to life. Rama immediately left in search of Shambuk.

Finally, Rama found Shambuk praying near a river in the forest. When Shambuk revealed his identity, Rama took out his sword and cut Shambuk's head off and the little boy became alive again.

## 7 A Case to Solve

Vikram was upset on hearing stories about the viciousness of men. Betal told him, "Okay, then let me tell you about a wicked woman."

Once there lived a rich man called Sagardati. He was a widower with a daughter named Mainashri. He was too busy to look after his daughter. So Mainashri began misusing her freedom. She made false promises to many men.

A man named Shridut loved her in spite of that. She decided to marry Shridut. However, after marriage she did not take any care of him and spent time with other men.

One night, she quietly slipped out of her house to meet a lover. Meanwhile, a thief had entered her lover's house and killed him. When Mainashri walked in, she found the man lying dead. A ghost

had been watching Mainashri's activities and decided to teach her a lesson. He revived the dead body and made it chop Mainashri's nose.

The wicked Mainashri returned home and blamed Shridut for whatever happened. All her neighbours took pity on her and called the police. After investigations, the police found the thief and caught him for the murder. When he told them the story about the

corpse biting Mainashri's nose, nobody believed him. Shridut was imprisoned for cutting off his wife's nose.

Now, Betal asked Vikram, "How would you have solved the case?" Vikram, who had judged many criminal cases, said, "I would have checked the corpse's mouth, for if it had bitten the nose, portions of flesh would still remain in its mouth."

"Brilliant," said Betal and disappeared again.

## 8 The War Ends

The Pandavas wanted to kill Ashvattama for the merciless manner in which he had killed their dear ones in the middle of the night. Draupadi was devastated since all her sons had been killed by Ashvattama. The Pandavas wanted revenge and searched for him and finally found him in Sage Vyasa's hermitage. Bhima fought a duel with Ashvattama and the latter finally accepted defeat.

The war finally ended after

eighteen days. Dhrithrashtra was devastated when he heard that Duryodhana had died. He was also furious when he heard how Ashvattama had killed Draupadi's sons. Vidura and Sage Vyasa consoled Dhrithrashtra by saying that the war had to happen. Gandhari too was very sad but blessed the Pandavas, who had emerged victorious.

Finally, the Pandavas went to the banks of the Ganga to perform the last rites of those who had lost their lives in the war.

## 9 Yudhishthira Is Crowned

The Pandavas had finally won the Mahabharata war and Yudhishthira was the rightful heir to the throne of Hastinapur now. But he felt that many people had lost their lives in the battle and he was not at peace with himself after the war and wanted to lead an ascetic life. His brothers tried to cheer him up and on Sage Vyasa's insistence and advice, Yudhishthira eventually agreed to take charge of Hastinapur.

An elaborate ceremony was arranged to crown Yudhisthira and declare him the new king of Hastinapur. The entire city was lit up. The palace was decorated and grand arrangements were made for the coronation ceremony. The people of the kingdom rejoiced and the sages blessed the new king. After his coronation, he went with Krishna to meet Bhishma who was lying on a bed of arrows on the battlefield. His brothers also accompanied him. Bhishma blessed Yudhishthira and advised him to always follow the path of truth and justice. Finally, Bhishma passed away peacefully and Yudhishthira returned to rule over his kingdom.

## 10 Krishna to the Rescue

The Pandavas were very angry with Ashvattama, Dronacharya's son, for setting their camp on fire. When Ashvattama saw the Pandavas approaching, he picked up a straw and ordered it to go and kill the baby of Abhimanyu and Uttara, who was still in Uttara's womb. The straw took the form of a sword. When Krishna saw the sword coming towards Uttara, he diffused its power and saved Uttara and her baby.

## 11 Krishna Meets Uttanka

Once Yudhisthira was crowned the king of Hastinapur, Krishna decided to return to Dwarka. On his way, he met a sage called Uttanka. He asked Krishna all about the war. Krishna told him everything. Uttanka was furious and thought that Krishna should have stopped the war. Krishna then appeared in his divine form and Uttanka was delighted. Krishna told him to ask for a boon. The sage said, "Whenever I want water, it should be available." Krishna blessed Uttanka and went away. Some days later, Uttanka was travelling across a desert and felt thirsty. Soon after, a man from a low caste appeared with water. Uttanka refused to accept water from him. Later, Krishna appeared and told Uttanka that the man was actually Indra in disguise. Uttanka was very ashamed of his behaviour.

## 12 The Demon with a Thousand Hands

Banasura, the demon, had a thousand hands with which he played the *mridanga*, while Shiva danced the *tandava*. Pleased with his talent, Shiva became his protector. Banasura became very arrogant and powerful after this. Banasura had a daughter named Usha. One day, she saw a man in her dream and fell in love with him. Usha's friend, Chitralekha, painted a picture of the man of Usha's dreams based on the description given by her. The picture resembled Anniruddha, Krishna's grandson. Usha asked her friend to help her get the man of her dreams. Chitralekha flew to Anniruddha and brought him to Usha. They fell in love with each other. Banasura did not approve of this and imprisoned Anniruddha.

Hearing this, Krishna came to rescue his grandson and fought Banasura. In the end Krishna defeated Banasura. Finally, at Shiva's request, Krishna spared Banasura's life but cut off his thousand hands, leaving only four.

# 13 Sita's Exile

Rama was a fair and just king and his people admired him for his wisdom and strength. One day, one of his spies told him that the people of Ayodhya were unhappy because they believed that he should not have accepted Sita after Ravana had kidnapped her. Rama was very sad but decided that he would have to send Sita away in order to keep his people happy.

Rama called for Laxmana and asked him to take Sita and leave her on the banks of the Ganga near Sage Valmiki's ashram. Laxmana was astonished at the request but could not disobey Rama. Next morning, Laxmana took Sita along with him to the river and told her that Rama had asked him to leave her there. Sita was shocked and fell unconscious. When she regained consciousness, she told Laxmana that she would do as Rama wishes and asked him to return. Laxmana left her with a heavy heart and returned to Ayodhya.

# 14 Luv and Kush

After the battle with Ravana, following Rama's instructions, Laxmana left Sita on the banks of the river Ganga. The pupils of Sage Valmiki saw her crying and told their guru.

Sage Valmiki realised that the woman was actually Sita and brought her to his ashram. From then on, Sita lived at the ashram of Sage Valmiki under his care. A few months later, she gave birth to twins. All the people at the ashram were happy because they had all grown very fond of Sita. Sage Valmiki named the two boys, Luv and Kush.

The twins stayed at the ashram and Sage Valmiki educated them.

Sage Valmiki knew that the boys would grow up and be as strong, wise, and intelligent as their father, Rama. He taught them archery and soon Luv and Kush became good warriors.

# 15 Krishna Dies

After the Mahabharata war ended and Yudhisthira was crowned the new and rightful king of Hastinapur, there were celebrations all over. Krishna bid farewell to the Pandavas and returned to Dwarka. He ruled over Dwarka for thirty-six years.

It is believed that one day, Krishna went to a forest and went off to sleep under a tree. Some time later, a hunter named Jara was passing through the forest.

Krishna was wearing yellow clothes and the soles of his feet were shining very brightly. The hunter mistook them to be the eyes of a deer. He aimed and shot a poisonous arrow, which pierced one of Krishna's feet. As soon as Jara realised what had happened, he rushed to Krishna and begged for forgiveness. Krishna assured Jara that this was destiny.

Then Vishnu's chariot appeared from the sky and Krishna sat in it and went to heaven.

# 16 The Journey to Heaven

After ruling over Hastinapur for many years, Yudhisthira wanted to leave the kingdom. Parikshit, Abhimanyu's son, was crowned the new king and the Pandavas and Draupadi set out for the Himalayas. They dressed like hermits and set out to visit many holy places across the country. Finally, they reached the foothills of the Himalayas and started climbing the mountains. Somewhere along the way, a dog started following them.

The Pandavas crossed many mountains and reached Himadri, the highest range of the mountains. The mountains were very steep and were covered with snow. The Pandavas started the difficult climb. Since it was difficult to walk on snow, Draupadi and all the Pandavas, except Yudhisthira, found it very difficult to continue on the journey. Draupadi was the first to fall to the ground and die on the way. She was followed by Sahadeva, Nakula, Arjuna, and finally Bhima. Only Yudhisthira and the dog adamantly continued marching ahead.

# 17 Luv and Kush and the White Horse

After Sita was sent away from Ayodhya by Rama, she lived in Sage Valmiki's ashram with her sons, Luv and Kush. The two boys grew up to be strong like their father, Rama.

One day, Rama held a big *Ashvamedha Yajna*. After the *yajna*, a sacred white horse was adorned with jewels and garments and it was declared that this horse would be taken around to many kingdoms across the region. A declaration was hung around the horse's neck, which stated that if anyone caught the horse, they would have to fight with the soldiers accompanying the horse. Shatrughana was entrusted with the task of taking the horse.

One day, the horse was passing by Sage Valmiki's ashram. Seeing the horse, Luv and Kush decided to take it to the ashram. While catching the horse, they noticed the declaration around its neck but were not in the least bit frightened. Soon, Shatrughana arrived with some soldiers and was furious to see that two young boys had caught the horse. He tried to persuade Luv and Kush to let the horse go but the boys were adamant and wanted to fight Shatrughana's army.

Luv and Kush were very good at archery, and soon Shatrughana's soldiers fled and he had to accept defeat.

Shatrughana went back and told Rama about the young boys and how they had defeated the army. Rama asked Laxmana to go to Valmiki's ashram and get the horse back from the boys. He told Laxmana to bring the boys to Ayodhya.

# 18 Luv and Kush Fight Laxmana

Luv and Kush defeated Shatrughana's army and refused to return the sacred horse. Hearing the news, Rama sent Laxmana to Valmiki's ashram to bring back the horse. However, Luv and Kush were stubborn and refused to part with the horse without a fight. Under Valmiki's guidance, Luv and Kush had become expert at archery and so were not afraid of Laxmana. A fight ensued between them and Laxmana. Kush promptly took his bow and arrow and sent an arrow flying toward Laxmana. Laxmana was furious and soon a fight between Laxmana on one hand, and Luv and Kush on the other, started.

Laxmana was very impressed with the strength and might of the two brothers. Luv and Kush shot many arrows at Laxmana and finally Laxmana was defeated and fell to the ground. Rama was shocked when he heard of Laxmana's fate. He summoned Bharata and told him to go to Valmiki's ashram with Hanuman.

# 19 Yudhishthira and the Faithful Dog

While Yudhisthira was walking towards the gates of heaven, a dog followed him. The other Pandavas, along with Draupadi, had died on the journey across the Himalayas, but the dog accompanied him throughout. Finally, Yudhisthira reached the gates of heaven. There, Indra appeared with a chariot and Yudhisthira mounted it. The dog was about to jump in too, but Indra got angry and declared that there was no place in heaven for a dog. Hearing this, Yudhisthira calmly got off the chariot and announced that he would not go to heaven unless the faithful dog was allowed to come along with him. Suddenly, the dog was transformed into Dharmaraja. He praised Yudhisthira for his wisdom and blessed him. Then Yudhisthira went to heaven.

# 20 Luv and Kush Meet Bharata

When Laxmana's army returned from Sage Valmiki's ashram after being defeated by Luv and Kush, Rama was amazed. He had never imagined that Laxmana would be defeated at the hands of such young lads. He quickly summoned Bharata and asked him to go and bring the two boys to Ayodhya immediately. He also advised Bharata to take Hanuman and the army of monkeys along with him for support.

When Luv and Kush saw Bharata along with his army, they were delighted to see so many monkeys. Soon, the battle began and Luv and Kush started shooting arrows at the monkey brigade. As the battle proceeded, even Bharata was forced to fall on the ground and surrender. Meanwhile, Hanuman, who was watching everything from a distance, realised that these young boys were not ordinary lads and recognised them as the brave sons of Rama and Sita.

## 21 Rama Meets His Sons

When Rama came to know about the defeat of Bharata and Hanuman at the hands of Luv and Kush, he decided to go to Sage Valmiki's ashram himself and meet the boys. When he reached the ashram and met Luv and Kush, he asked them who they were. Luv replied that they were the children of Vanadevi, as Sita was known in the ashram. They said that Sage Valmiki had educated them.

As soon as Rama heard this, he realised that these brave young boys were his own sons. In the meantime, Luv and Kush started shooting arrows at Rama and his army. Just then, Sage Valmiki appeared. He told the boys that Rama was actually their father. Rama hugged his children and wept with joy.

## 22 The Talented Brothers

As Vikram carried Betal on his back, he narrated another story. Two very talented brothers, Som and Mangal, lived in the kingdom of Jaisingh. The first one had very powerful eyesight and the second one had a strong sense of smell. King Jaisingh made them his guards.

One day, the neighbouring king invited Jaisingh to his kingdom. Jaisingh sensed that there was a risk to his life, so he took the two brothers with him. After a grand dinner, Jaisingh was taken to his bedroom. As he was about to go to sleep, Som spotted a thorn on his bed. When Mangal smelled the thorn he said that it was poisonous and if Jaisingh had slept on it, he would have died. Betal asked Vikram, "Which brother was more talented?" Vikram answered, "Som was more talented because his talent saved the king's life." Betal said, "This is the right answer." He flew away because Vikram had spoken.

## 23 Yudhisthira Passes the Test

Indra took Yudhisthira to heaven in his chariot. As soon as he stepped into heaven, he was surprised to see Duryodhana there and he asked Indra how a person like him could be in heaven. Yudhisthira couldn't see Draupadi and his brothers anywhere and he questioned Indra about them. Indra called a guard and asked him to take Yudhisthira to his brothers and Draupadi. The guard took Yudhisthira through a foul-smelling path strewn with the bodies of dead animals. Yudhisthira was finding it very difficult to follow the guard but did not say a word. Suddenly, he heard some cries and familiar sounds. He heard a voice saying, "I am Bhima" and another one said, "I am Abhimanyu." Yudhisthira realised that his brothers and wife were in hell. Furious to see his loved ones suffering he said, "I have no right to live in heaven while my loved ones are suffering here."

Suddenly, Dharmaraja appeared and the foul smell changed to a sweet fragrance. He blessed Yudhisthira and said that he had put Yudhisthira through a test by showing him that his brothers and Draupadi were suffering in hell. Since Yudhisthira had decided to stay with them in hell, Dharmaraja had come to bless Yudhisthira in person. He continued, saying, "None of your loved ones are in hell. This is just an illusion to test you. You have always been an ideal king and it is essential for you to see the suffering people go through in hell." Yudhisthira was delighted to hear that his brothers and Draupadi were in heaven and he joined them there.

## 24 Bholu and the Giant

As Vikram carried Betal, he told him another story.

In the kingdom of King Kiripal lived a big giant who used to eat people. All the people were terrified. The king announced that whoever could kill the giant would get the princess's hand in marriage as a reward. Many people tried to win the reward but were killed by the demon. One day, an ordinary village boy, Bholu, killed the giant. The king did not want to marry his daughter to him. So, he declared that Bholu would be given a test before he got the reward. But Bholu refused to take any reward. The princess insisted that she would marry Bholu.

Betal asked Vikram, "Why did they act in that way?" Vikram replied, "Bholu declined the reward because he had killed the giant for the welfare of people. The princess declared to marry Bholu to keep her father's word." Betal heard this and flew away.

## 25 The Earth Shelters Sita

Rama finally met his sons. As Sita watched their meeting from a distance, Rama's eyes fell on her. He became sad because he wasn't sure if the people of Ayodhya would accept Sita as their queen as she had stayed with *rakshasis* for such a long time. Sage Valmiki urged Rama to take Sita and the children back to Ayodhya. Rama loved Sita, but his duty towards the people of Ayodhya came first. He refused to take Sita. Sita decided to return to Mother Earth. She appealed, "Oh, Mother Earth, if you think that I have not committed any sin, please take me in your lap and give me a place." Suddenly the earth split into two. Seated on a beautiful throne, Mother Earth emerged from inside the earth. She took Sita in her lap and descended back into the earth. Luv and Kush cried for their mother to come back. There were tears in Rama's eyes as well. But Sita was gone forever.

## 26 Yamaraj Meets Rama

After ruling Ayodhya for many years, Rama became tired and wanted to go to heaven. Vishnu realised this and asked Yamaraj to go and bring Rama. Yamaraj disguised himself as a sage and went to Ayodhya. He met Laxmana at the entrance to Rama's chamber and ordered him not to allow anyone inside while he talked to Rama. On meeting Rama, Yamaraj told him that he had come to take Rama to heaven. Meanwhile, Sage Durvasa came to the palace and ordered Laxmana to allow him to meet Rama. Laxmana refused. Enraged at this, Durvasa cursed Laxmana to leave the earth and go to heaven. But when, Durvasa saw Rama with Yamaraj, he realised his mistake. Meanwhile, Laxmana had been cursed to die, and so he went and jumped in the river. Rama was grief-stricken by his brother's death.

## 27 Curse on Parikshit

Abhimanyu's son, Parikshit became the king of Hastinapur after the Pandavas left for the mountains.

One day, while wandering in a forest, Parikshit felt thirsty. He came upon a sage and asked him for some water. The sage was meditating and did not hear Parikshit. Losing his temper, the king lifted a dead snake and put it on the shoulders of the sage like a garland. Just then, the sage's son returned and saw the king do this. He was furious and cursed Parikshit to die from a snakebite within seven days. The sage scolded his son and sent a message to the king informing him about the curse. Soon, a big palace was built for Parikshit where he could be safe from snakes.

However, on the seventh day, the king of serpents, Takshaka, disguised himself as a worm and entered a fruit. As soon as the king bit the fruit, Takshaka assumed his real form and coiled himself around Parikshit, killing him.

## 28 The Snake Sacrifice

After the death of Parikshit, his son Janmejaya became the king of Hastinapur. Janmejaya wanted to avenge his father's death and wanted to kill Takshaka. He decided to organise a snake sacrifice. Accordingly, a sacrificial fire was burnt where the holy priests chanted the names of different snakes.

As a result, the snakes became powerless and fell into the sacrificial fire one by one and perished. The great snake sacrifice continued for many days and hundreds and thousands of snakes emerged from everywhere and surrendered to the sacrificial fire. Everyone waited for Takshaka but he was missing. Everyone, including the priests and Janmejaya were puzzled, as they did not know that Takshaka had gone to Indra for protection.

# 29 Astika Saves Takshaka

To avenge his father's death at the hands of Takshaka, the king of serpents, Janmejaya held a snake sacrifice. Mantras were chanted to destroy the snakes but Takshaka did not appear. The head priests thought that Takshaka had sought protection from Indra. They chanted a special mantra to compel Takshaka to appear and fall in the sacrificial fire along with Indra. Soon, both Takshaka and Indra appeared and fell into the fire together. When Indra saw that Takshaka was bound to die, he deserted him.

Meanwhile, Jaratkaru, Takshaka's younger sister, ordered her son, Astika, to save Takshaka. Astika approached Janmejaya and requested him for a boon. He said that the snake sacrifice had led to the death of millions of snakes and if Janmejaya spared the remaining few, including Takshaka, he will be glorified. Sage Vyasa advised Janmejaya to grant Astika's request and end the snake sacrifice. He agreed and thus, Takshaka was saved.

# 30 Rama Goes to Heaven

Rama's loyal brother, Laxmana had been cursed by Sage Durvasa and had gone to heaven. Rama could not bear this loss. He decided to go to heaven himself. He wanted to crown Bharata as the king of Ayodhya, but both Bharata and Shatrughna felt that they were not the rightful successors to the throne.

Rama wanted to know what the people of Ayodhya wanted. The people of Ayodhya loved Rama and announced that they would also accompany Rama to heaven. Rama had to agree to their wish. He bid a tearful farewell to his faithful devotee, Hanuman, and blessed him. Then, he went to the banks of the Saryu River and walked into the water. The people of Ayodhya, who had been accompanying Rama all the while, followed their king and went to heaven.

# 31 A Brave Boy

Betal told Vikram, "You are a brave warrior, but let me tell you the story of a brave boy."

Once there lived a king called Jairajan. One day he discovered that his relatives were planning to steal his throne and kill him. To avoid bloodshed, Jairajan gave up his crown and went to live in a far-off village. Here he married a girl and started living happily.

One day, while returning home he saw a pile of human bones lying on the path. Shocked, he hurried back home and told his wife about the incident. She told him that the wicked king of the kingdom was sacrificing young boys to the eagle, Garuda. Jairajan found out that the next time, a boy named Shankar was going to be fed to the eagle. He met Shankar's parents and offered to sacrifice his life instead, though Shankar protested.

On the day of the sacrifice, Garuda whisked Jairajan away. Shankar risked his life and ran to save Jairajan, but he was killed. When the news reached Jairajan's wife she begged Garuda to return her husband. Seeing her devotion, Garuda gave back Jairajan's life. Jairajan now prayed to Garuda to revive all the other corpses. The eagle fulfilled his wish.

Now Betal put forward the question, "Whose sacrifice was greater, Shankar's or Jairajan's?" Vikram promtly replied, "Shankar. Though he was a mere boy he volunteered to sacrifice his own life." Since Vikram had opened his mouth again, Betal flew away.